Cowboy'n
The Way It Was

by Oley Kohlman

Other books by Oley Kohlman

Whiff of Sage

Moonshiners, Bootleggers, and Some Prohibition

Uphill with the Ski Troops

Second Opinion

Library of Congress Catalog Number
ISBN 1-879894-06-8

Library of Congress Catalog Card No.
94-79231

Illustrations by Bill Culbertson
Cover design by Jerry Palen

My cowboy days were not wasted. To those people that have to put a dollar value on each day of their lives, *don't become a cowboy!*

I rode for wages starting part time in 1934 and kept on until 1942 when I took out 34 months and one day to serve my country. From a financial standpoint I did not get rich living the life of Riley, but reading this will give you a sample of the rewards that I did enjoy.

—Oley Kohlman

Acknowledgments

Thanks to my wife, Grace, who suggested that I write this book. Also thanks for the editing, correcting punctuation, and encouraging that helped get it done.

Thanks to Deanna Berry for the use of the old Johnson photo albums. Also thanks to Hilda Van Valkenburg for the picture of me.

Thanks to Bill Culbertson for the illustrations.

Thanks to Jack Kisling for the introduction.

Last but not least, thanks to Laffing Cow Press.

Thanks to Jerry Palen for designing the cover. Thanks to Ann Palen for her always helpful editing.

Thanks to Susannah Borg for her expertise and thanks to Keith McLendon for scattering the whole thing together.

And to all those who helped that I forgot to mention… Thanks!

Introduction

In some people, turning nouns into verbs is a bad habit. In others it's a gift.

Oley Kohlman is one of the others, and as you read *Cowboy'n* you'll discover that it isn't easy to cowboy and it isn't easy to describe it either. Sailors sail, sawyers saw, and cowboys cowboy.

Starting in the early 30's, Kohlman cowboyed in North Park, that high, wide, and handsome patch of Colorado that's a little to the right of the Continental Divide and just south of Wyoming.

The world, as Oley knew it then, consisted of two parts: North Park and "Outside;" and the year was divided into two seasons: Fourth of July and winter. North Park was livestock country and under the newly-passed Taylor Grazing Act 100,000 acres of it was open range where Oley, a young transplant from the eastern plains, was paid a cool $30 a month to disturb cattle.

The work was hard, the hours were long, and so was winter. From Thanksgiving on, horse-drawn sleds were the only reliable way to haul cargo. Skis were for transportation, not fun, and snow was a certainty you didn't fight. You just lived with it. Once, on a trip to the "Outside," Oley was amazed to see people shoveling snow off Denver streets. You didn't catch North Park people doing such dumb things.

In these pages you'll meet a lot of cow horses, a lot of cow folks and even a few sheep folks. Sheep folks? Sure. Flying in the face of fiction, Oley says sheep folks and cow folks get along fine. "I always liked being with them," he says.

Among other things, Oley tells how, in a world where castrating another man's bull was a prison offense, a couple of glass door knobs could come in handy. And how to keep things warm when it's so cold that kerosene freezes. And why, for cowboy'n purposes, muddy water quenches thirst just about as well as clear.

–Jack Kisling

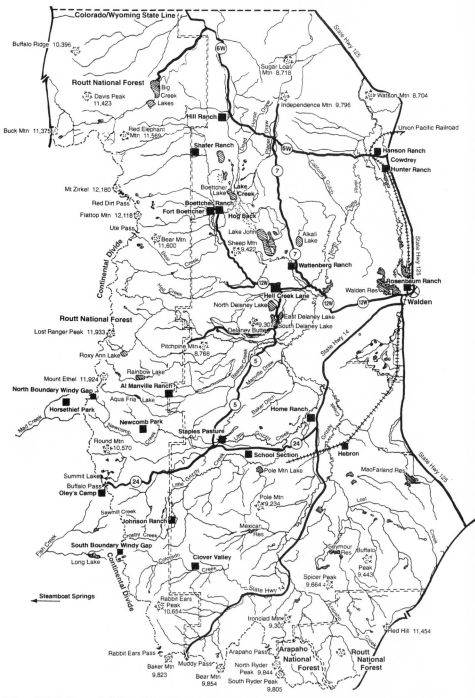

The Vicinity of The Big Horn Ranches of Jackson County circa 1934

■ Ranch or Point of Interest		–··–··– Continental Divide
▨ Lake or Reservoir		⌇⌇⌇⌇ National Park Boundary
∿ Roads	COLORADO	☼ Mountain with elevation
— Creeks, Draws, & Rivers	Mile N	⤬ Mountain Pass

"A neighbor had a Red Durham bull that was in the habit of visiting our cows. There was no market for Brockley faced bulls in those Hereford days so when we caught that bull in our cows we roped it and tied it down. Jack (White) took out his pocketknife and handed it to me and said 'Here, you cut him!' When neither of us would, it being a penitentiary offense to cut a bull on the Open Range, Jack rode off saying he'd be back."

"Jack came back alright and with a pair of glass door knobs that his mother had sent to him. Well, we made a quick change, applied some stitches and had no more Brockley faced off-spring!"

—as told by Ferrington Carpenter about his and Jack White's purebred operation in 1909.

A New Way of Life

Here is a little history of what has happened to the grass in North Park in the last 114 years. In 1879 William Trownsell, my wife's grandfather homesteaded on the ranch that we own today. I have pieced this history together from documents that were handed down, from my own experiences, and from just listening to old timers since coming to North Park 60 years ago.

In 1879 North Park was wild-game country. Buffalo, elk, deer, and antelope were plentiful as were the Indians that came in the summer to hunt. The two main tribes that hunted North Park were the Utes and the Arapahos. The Crows, Sioux, and Cheyennes were also known to frequent this country. There were fierce battles fought among the tribes over this prime hunting ground. In 1879 the Meeker Massacre took place and the Utes were moved out. The Indian era was over.

White men came early to trap and mine, but in 1878 there were several bunches of cattle brought into North Park for summer grazing. William Trownsell was here that year, then came back the next year and homesteaded. The situation then has been described as follows: bunchgrass was everywhere, very little sagebrush, very few willows, and no trout.

Going into the 1880's there was still lots of wild game which attracted market hunters who took out wagon-loads of game to sell in Leadville, Laramie, and Denver. Market hunters continued this practice for several years until the game was finally depleted.

From the start, ranchers developed meadows with irrigation systems and filed on water rights so they could put in hay for winter feeding.

In the early 1880's huge bunches of steers were brought into North Park, as there was big boom in the cattle business. Prices were good, grass was free, and there was a big influx of English as well as Eastern money.

I was told by one of the first ranchers that operated in North Park that they fed between 60 and 90 days. In the Spring, as soon as there were bare spots showing up on the south slopes, they would take the cattle where the bunchgrass was heavy and well-cured. Then as the need arose, they would breaks trails to new feed. As the grass greened up the cattle moved up into the mountains where they summered. As the snow came in the fall they moved back down.

The steer outfits not only summered in North Park, they wintered here too! They got by until the winter of 1886 when a hard winter wiped most of them out. Whoever did survive was done in by the winter of 1887. After that no one tried to winter cattle in North Park without feeding hay.

But the damage was done. Most of the bunchgrass had been over grazed and thinned, never to return as it had been. The sagebrush took over as the dominant plant on large portions of the North Park range.

Please remember that a marketable critter then consisted of a steer that weighed over 1,000 pounds. Many steers reached that weight at 2 years, some had to be kept 3 or even 4 years before they reached that weight.

In 1889 Granpaw Trownsell trailed 80 head of steers to Laramie, Wyoming and shipped from there by railroad to

Omaha, Nebraska. Average weight of 1,160 pounds brought from $1.95 to $2.60 per hundred pound. They netted $23.10 per head after $4.76 a head was taken out for shipping and expenses!

All work, freighting and travelling, was done by horsepower. Every rancher had a horse herd that lived on the free range. There was a horse roundup each year before haying when the colts would be branded and cut. Then the hay horses would be kept in and the rest turned out on the free range.

There were several horse outfits here in the early days: the Cross Brothers, the Knox-Percheron, and Charles Boettcher.

People were also busy homesteading. When Teller City gave up the ghost in 1883, many people from there took up homesteads. A homestead consisted of 160 acres until 1912 when 320 acres could be filed on. There were desert claims and rock claims, as well as tree claims. Claims cost $1.00 to $1.50 per acre, along with a person's ability to meet certain requirements. Then in 1916, a whole section (640 acres) could be filed on. These became known as grazing homesteads.

Around the turn of the century the Colorado Cattlemen's Association had advocated a homestead of 2,560 acres so that a rancher would have a chance of a ranch really working.

In 1891 Congress authorized the President the power to set aside areas of National Forest for control of grazing and timber (politics ain't changed much). No funds were supplied to administer these areas, but that did not stop various presidents from withdrawing some 40 million acres by 1904.

About that time the Colorado Cattleman's Association was split between paying a grazing fee on public land or maintaining free range. The State of Colorado tried to help and was able to declare large tracts of land as State School Lands and lease the same for grazing.

There was a great hue and cry for public lands to be sold into private ownership and the pressure was on. Congress acted in 1904 and moved the National Forest out of the Interior

Department and into the Agricultural Department where it was finally funded.

The ranchers of North Park submitted to control of numbers and paid a fee for grazing on the National Forest, but not many willingly.

In 1913 the railroad came to North Park, so there was no longer a need to trail cattle to Laramie.

During and following WWI cattle prices boomed then broke along with the banks. Many cattlemen went broke and ended up in the sheep business which took a lot of vitriol out of bringing sheep into North Park. So sheep came into North Park a lot quieter than was the case west across the Divide.

In 1934, in the midst of the Depression, there was a drought with very little hay being raised in North Park and a cattle market that is impossible to believe today. All cattle were shipped to market by railroad, many times a car of cattle would not pay expenses.

By the fall of 1934 there was no market and very little hay in North Park. The United States Government came in and paid something like $6 for a calf and around $12 for a cow, then had people go around and shoot them and leave them lay.

There you have a look at the situation just after I started riding for The Big Horn outfit in the Spring of 1934. The year that The Taylor Act was passed that was to end the free range in North Park forever.

To say that the free range was a disaster would be an understatement! To those of you who harp about the range going downhill, *you were not there when free range ended!* No way has the range in North Park ever been in as sad shape any time since 1934!

What do I base that statement on? I rode the range from 1934 through 1941, then 4 years out for service in WWII, then rode for 5 years through 1950.

What do I mean by riding? There were no cattle guards when I started and no horse trailers. We rode wherever we went.

Cowboys on The Big Horn in those days fixed no fence and pitched no manure or hay except in the winters. Then if we were where they had calves we would pitch the hay up a couple times a day. We each had a string of 6 or 7 horses we kept shod ourselves. The hay was put up and fed out on contract with generally 400 cows to a bunch fed by one man with a pitchfork every day.

Now you know why.

The free range before The Taylor Act was crowded with cattle, sheep, and horses there to eat the grass as soon as it showed up. Really the ranchers of North Park did not handle the free range any better than the steer outfits had in the 1880's.

The Taylor Act was passed to administer some 142 million acres of Public Domains in the western United States—142 million acres that were left over after everyone had picked it over for homesteads, the bottom of the barrel!

Ferrington Carpenter of Hayden was chosen to set up the rules to allot this land between the cattlemen and the sheepmen. This included the transient rancher who owned no land and ran on Government land entirely unlike The Big Horn that had been on the range for 55 years when The Taylor Act was passed.

There was a crew of 16 people that set up all of the allotments and settled the differences between the sheepmen and the cattlemen. They settled a lot of knotty problems and set the first fee at 5¢ per A.U.M. (Animal Unit per Month). They sent out the first statement for the 1937 grazing season. I felt that those 16 people divided the Public Domains in North Park fairly. How many people would it take today to do that?

Range recovery has been slow, but steady. I can state firmly however, that there is no part of the North Park Range that is not better today than in 1934 or 1937 when it was first administered. So if it ain't broke don't fix it.

When I came to North Park in July of 1933 I was 21 years old. I came from a dry-land outfit, which was mostly dry farming, cattle, milk cows, bucket calves, hogs, chickens, and horses to do the farming. I had broke horses both to work and to ride. I had also tried calf roping and bareback and bronc riding, without a lot of success

I came to hay for Otto Johnson. My brother Dutch hayed for Billy and Little Bill Heinemen where he stacked hay and got $1.50 a day. I worked broncs in the hay field and got $1.25 a day. At that time the going wage was $1 a day and board so we were pretty lucky.

The day we arrived at Johnsons, Dr. Cunningham had stopped on his way back to Coalmont. He said he had been up to Clover Valley at The Big Horn cow camp where he had taped up Bert Wilcox's broken ribs, the result of fly time. Bert was leading a packhorse loaded with salt. The lead rope managed to get under Bert's mount's tail and the horse bucked him off and stepped on him.

The father of the Johnson family, Otto, was known as "Pop" while his wife, Ida, was called "Maw." Their sons were Walter, known as "Curley," Delmar known as "Del" who was born in 1900 (Del was 33 years old when I met him), and Durward, the oldest who was a Forest Ranger in Middle Park. Altho' the "boys" had a fox farm and a sawmill, everybody helped in haying.

That summer Curley Johnson and I spent many a rainy afternoon playing a bit of penny-ante with The Big Horn cowboys in Clover Valley. In the fall of 1933 The Big Horn bought hay from the Johnsons and I helped to feed it out. The cowboys were often there while I worked and several times I rode with them and got to know them.

Haying in North Park in the 1930's was horsepower by horses! If there were any tractors used, and there might have been, I never saw them.

The Johnsons had 2 horse-drawn mowers, probably a 5-foot cutter bar, a 12-foot rake pulled by a team, and a 10-foot rake with shafts so it was a one-horse rake. A sweep, a slide, and a pusher were the other equipment used.

The Johnsons as I met them in 1933. Pop, Del, Curley, Maw, and the dog, Pat,

The mowers were pulled by two horses. We used the mowers to work the broncs with an older horse after we had driven them on a wagon several times. The rake team were smaller horses, and the team rake was the head-rake, whereas the one horse rake was used for scatter raking and cleaning up around the stack.

I came from rattlesnake country and grew up with them. When I first came to North Park I had a problem. Those wild Iris (or flags) had seed pods that dried out and split with the seeds loose inside. When they were shook they rattled like a rattlesnake, close enough that it took me several years to get use to it. North Park never had rattlesnakes until they were brought in by one S.A. McIntyre better known as "Rattlesnake Jack" who was a famous wolf trapper. The story was that he had been in a sideshow, and always had rattlesnakes in a glass box. He tried to get them started here but the North Park climate took care of one more nuisance.

Meals were good, three hot meals a day. I knew of some outfits that hired a fisherman to catch trout to feed the hay crew. There were lots of sage grouse and they were easy to get.

Most ranches butchered a beef, and the larder was always full of fresh groceries. The custom was to buy groceries twice a year, once for haying and once for a winter order.

These orders were for all staples: flour and sugar by the 100-pound sacks, coffee by the 3- or 5-pound cans, cases of all canned goods, along with 25-pound boxes of dried fruit and prunes make up a partial list. It seemed that every ranch wife took a great deal of pride in feeding whoever came to her table.

Early in the morning wrangling the horses was the most uncomfortable job. At Johnsons the horse pasture was all timber and it was always cold. A sheepskin coat and a pair of overshoes (even in July and August) was the usual. Those old horses were wise and hard to find, and would slip off from the bunch. Quite a challenge for a prairie raised, dry-lander. That was my first experience in brush popping and it stood me in good stead later on.

The open snowless falls gave me trouble. Mornings my feet would get cold, so cold that I would put on my overshoes. Then when it would warm up I got kidded about wearing out my overshoes before winter got there.

A trick that I discovered. Before winter I'd take a piece of inner tube about a foot long and as wide as my stirrup, put it around the stirrup, and rivet a piece of leather on each side. That way snow and ice never built up in my stirrups.

Johnsons had cribs for all the hay, about 12 by 16 feet with 8 foot sides, where all the hay was stacked. With cribs the stacks did not have to be fenced, and the edges did not get frozen in during the winter. A good stack was 10 ton.

It was a toss-up which was the lowliest job on the hay crew,

A crib of hay.

the raker or the chore boy. The scatter raker's job was to clean up after everyone in the hay field, while the chore boy milked the cows, ground the mower sickles, and helped the cook, maybe not in the kitchen, but he would help take the hot lunch to the field at noon. It was not unusual for the ranch wife to have a hired girl during haying either.

By today's standards haying at Johnsons in 1933 was slow, around two stacks a day. We did not take big loads. I did all the sweeping with the same team, and we used a 2-horse team on the pusher. The whole operation only took about a dozen horses. In the 30's The Big Horn contracted the haying on their ranches at the rate of $2 a ton, and 50¢ a ton for feeding it out.

So, in the fall of 1933, when The Big Horn bought hay from Johnsons, they paid either $3 or $3.25 a ton fed out. When haying was finished Pop Johnson made me an offer: if I would come back for the winter, and feed one load of hay a day, I could have the rest of the day off to trap, and he would give me overall money in the spring. It sounded good to me because I had trapped some as I grew up.

After we had gathered the crops at home, I came back to Johnsons to learn a new way of life, being "snowed in" all winter long!

What did being "snowed in" mean? In 1933 if Jackson County had any snow plowing equipment it was used to keep the road to Laramie open. That was the only road kept open for many years. If the road was closed, no problem, the train came from Laramie on Monday, Wednesday, and Friday. It went back on Tuesday, Thursday, and Saturday. The train was the only carrier of the U.S. Mail in those days. In other words there was no attempt to use any roads after it "snowed up."

The custom was that everyone put their cars in their garage, jacked them up, put blocks under them to hold them up to keep the tires from rotting, and left them there until the spring mud had dried up. Therefore all traveling was done by horses and sleds, or horseback. Cross country skiing was not popular in North Park in 1933 but it was the first year that I skied.

Being snowed in was a rather peaceful, good feeling that you were secure and had everything that you would need. We did get mail by the neighbors bringing it part way. We kept a snow trail broke out to the next neighbors, that was Stanbaughs, a good 2 miles, the next was Turners another mile and a half. That was where we generally got the mail, either of those places. There were no telephones, but we did have a radio of sorts at Johnsons. Still we had no way to know when somebody had been down to Coalmont and had gotten mail for us.

For entertainment I read. It seems I read most everything available. They didn't take many magazines or papers but they

Beards on Otto Johnson and I. Mud Season 1934.

took *National Geographic* magazine. Del must have had ten years of back issues, all of which I read. Pop and I also used to play cards, two games an evening. I don't recall having listened to much on the radio, KSL Salt Lake and KOA Denver were some of the stations that we could get, but none of them came in good at night. I do recall listening to Admiral Bird at the South Pole once tho'.

"Outside" was a term used back then that you hear less and less of. Whenever one was going out of North Park, be it to Laramie, Fort Collins, or Denver, you were going outside. I never went outside that first winter. I never went as far as Coalmont. That was a change from going to dances every Saturday night as we had been doing at home.

Oh by the way, Johnsons had something rare for 1933, a modern bathroom. They had piped a spring into the house years before and had a stool and a bathtub with hot and cold running water. There was a Delco Light Plant so we had electric lights too.

Sure Johnsons had an indoors bathroom, but they also had a backhouse. That was standard on all ranches in North Park.

It was complete with catalogs as toilet paper did not come into general use until indoor plumbing came along.

Maw Johnson gave us all hair cuts as needed. In the winter of 1933 and 1934 Pop Johnson grew a beard. He said it kept his face warm. I being 21 years old tried to grow my first beard and had only medium success. I had let my hair grow most of the winter. Towards spring Maw insisted she give me a hair cut. To keep peace in the house I consented. After she had cut what she thought was needed I looked in the mirror, and saw a beard topped out with a pinhead.

At Johnsons we never changed the bath routine. It was every Saturday night, as I had been brought up. Maw did the laundry and had a Maytag washer and wringer. Clothes drying was done on a clothes line out doors although I'm sure lots of our under-wear were dried in the house. Here I'd better explain, we never shoveled paths, we kept a pair of webs or snowshoes handy and instead of shovelling we tramped trails wherever we needed to go. Out under the clothesline was a must.

Life with the Johnsons was a change too. Altho they only bought groceries twice a year, the larder was well stocked. For meat we lived on wild game, deer or elk, and none of either wintered in North Park in those days. We had a meat house where we hung them, and they stayed frozen all winter. To-wards spring when we would run out of game, we would butcher a beef, boy did it ever taste good! Johnsons always had a spud patch and there was a root cellar under the cabin with the trap door in the living room. We always milked a cow or two, and Maw had home-canned fruit. Other vegetables were bought canned. I'll say this tho', Maw was an exceptional cook. We lived on wild game for months, but it was always different, how she did it I'll never know.

Despite the fact that Maw did a great job cooking, wild meat can get rather monotonous. None of the Johnsons were pickle eaters, but for a little extra flavor, there was a goodly patch of horseradish around. I would dig the roots and grind

them indoors with a hand grinder. Boy, was it ever strong! I'd shed many tears before I would get a quart or so ground. But I was always glad I had done it before the winter was done. And when the deer and elk were gone, horseradish helped the beef too.

We boys, Curley, Del and I, slept in the bunkhouse until after the new house was finished. The bunkhouse was made of logs, set out about a hundred feet back of the house. Del did not like to sleep in a warm room, so we each had a bed with around six quilts on top. We would not build a fire in the woodstove until the frost had crept down next to us. It would first show up between the top quilts and progress down. We'd live with the frost about a week before we would build a fire, tear our beds apart, and dry them out. We never tarried when we went out of the house to go to bed, we went right to bed! Likewise, in the mornings we got up, dressed, and headed straight for the house. It was cold, but we slept well. That was sure enough good training for me later when I got into the Ski Troops.

On Sunday evenings we almost always had oyster stew. Maw Johnson was something else! She had her own milk cows. After haying, I had offered to milk the cows, but she always said "No, I milk my own cows."

She insisted on milking her cows until one evening Maw had been to town and got home late. I suggested again I'd be glad to do the milking and that time she agreed. I milked the cows and brought the milk into the house. She hurried over, looked into the bucket, and said, "You get as much milk as I do, those boys don't." From then on I milked Maw Johnson's cows.

A bit of background. The Johnson's ranch was the end of the road in Crosby Draw. South you could get thru to Clover Valley, but nobody lived year around above. They were the last ranch to put up hay. As the crow flies we called it 3 miles down to Turners, in the winter there was generally 3 feet less snow in those three miles. It was 4 or 5 miles west to the top of the Continental Divide and lots of snow. The snow trail that everybody used went down the creeks, not down the lanes as in summer, because the feed trails of the different ranches tended to be along the creeks, where the hay was.

What was a snow trail? As one went by sled, the horses packed the snow. Every time it snowed, you went over and

The Johnsons as they left Pierce in 1914. Otto driving with Delmer and Ida in Back

packed it again. If a foot or two of snow fell, everything would look alike. To keep track of where the trail was, we would cut willow branches about three feet long and stick them in the snow right along the side of the sled. When those got almost covered up, it was time to remark the trail.

The Johnsons homesteaded in North Park in 1914. They had come from near Pierce, Colorado, where they had worked an irrigated farm for several years. My Dad and Otto Johnson got acquainted when they both worked for a horse dealer, Gus Ballard, who had a stable in Denver, and bought and sold horses. Gus also bought horses to ship east and south. My Dad told of how, when they were roping horses, they would bet a dime a throw, miss and pay, catch and win. He said after Otto Johnson was there a short time they quit that because Otto never missed! He was the best at fore-footing a horse that I ever saw. For many years he had made a business of castrating horses. He would forefoot them, throw them, and tie them down for the operation. Charge was $2.

Pop used to always get a rise out of Maw by referring to Crosby Draw as Poverty Hollow. When Johnsons were first on the homestead they worked several winters for Andy Norell. Maw cooked and the boys fed cattle and did ranch work.

I know that they were there during World War I because Maw told of rationing and all the off-breed flour, such as rye and barley, that one had to buy to be eligible to buy regular wheat flour. Andy hid all the off-breed flour in the attic and then when the war was over they fed it to the pigs.

Andy also kept and raised hogs. One time Norell was going to Stock Show and left a sow that was due to furrow with Anton Verner who was working there at the time. The last thing Norell said, "Vern, you save those pigs!"

As it usually is during Stock Show time, it turned cold, like 30 or 40 below zero, and those piglets all froze stiff. When Norell came home the first thing he did was to go look in the hog house. When he couldn't find any pigs he said," Vern, I told you to save those pigs!"

Vern said, "I did." He had driven nails around the inside of the hog house where he had hung up each of those frozen pink pigs. Saved!

The Johnsons homesteaded the original 160 acres in 1914, where the buildings are. They bought the Adam Gottler place about 1920, when they could not agree on the boundary line between them. The original survey of North Park left a lot to be desired in accuracy. I am not sure when the Johnsons acquired the Kinsniaw place on Chedsey Creek, but they later traded it to Raymond Rosses' mother for the half section North of the Bennett place that the Johnsons bought from the Andy Norell estate in the late 1920's.

The old Bennett place belonged to the Bennett, of Bennett and Wells, who had a sawmill at the foot of Buffalo Pass. In 1933 the Bennett house still stood. As was the custom, the walls were papered with newspapers. Some dated from 1898 and told of the Spanish-American War.

The water rights in Bennett Lake came with the Norell deal. I am not sure about the dam below Hidden Lake. It came either with the Gottler or Norell deal. Added in the early 1920's was Mexican Ridge, from Stanbaughs to Clover Valley. The three Johnson brothers homesteaded, Delmer on the north, Walter in the middle, and Durward on the south, also Otto, the father, was able to file on an additional three quarters of a section. Each got a section, 640 acres.

I have talked about having to go to the neighbors for the mail. That was generally the case, but Johnsons did go down country several times a winter. Del went outside, as well as to Walden, on business, and always brought the mail when he came back, along with everyone else's mail along the trail.

We did not always go for the mail with a team and sled, generally only when the trail needed packing. After I learned to ski in the fall of 1933, I would hitch up a dog sled to go get the mail, as there was generally an order from Monkey Wards that was too much to get into my small backpack. We did not have ruck sacks yet.

Del and Curley had a fox farm where they raised silver foxes and ranch mink. They had bought their start from Wayne Light in Steamboat about 1930 or '31. By 1933 they must have had 20 pairs of foxes, and a dozen pens of mink. Each pair of foxes had to have a pen separate from other foxes, these pens were chicken-wire pens about 25 feet wide by 100 feet long, covered on top, with the wire dug down around the edges, so the floor was not entirely covered with wire as the sides were. Each pen had two nest boxes that were about three feet above the ground. They were back to back, but the entrances were at opposite sides because foxes got riled up. When they had pups they moved. If there was not anywhere to move to, they would carry those pups around until they would die. To keep from losing the pups, they would watch how the old foxes acted when they had pups in the spring. After about 4 weeks they would open up the nest box, give the pups a worm pill, and treat their

A fox up on the nest box at the fox farm.

ears for ear mites. Then they would let the old vixen move the pups.

There was an ice house, a meat house, and a complete butcher shop for the fox farm. They fed horse meat to the foxes and mink, along with ground bone, and the hides with the hair left on and chopped up into small squares. They fed cod liver oil and cereal that I can recall. While there was snow on they did not have to water the animals. In summer they had to water and feed every day. Any fox food left over was not offered again. I do not recall if the mink were that particular. The pens had to be cleaned regularly. Today we would say it was a labor intensive operation. The going rate for fox horses was $5 a head. It varied, but the foxes would eat a horse about every two or three weeks in the fall when the pups were growing. Then after the pups were pelted around the first of November, the food consumption went down. Mink did not eat much compared to foxes and were pelted about the same time.

This is sort of how they operated. They would buy probably 15 horses in the fall and keep them until it got to freezing hard. Then they would butcher enough horses to run thru the winter, quarter them, and hang them up frozen in the fox farm meat house. As they were needed they would thaw a quarter and process it. They always wintered several fox horses to have some to use after it started to thaw in the spring. Fox horses were bought locally, some were old, some crippled, and some were outlaws.

As there was always lots of fox feed available, it was dog heaven. The Johnsons had Pat, a police dog, and I believe a police bitch that raised a litter of pups now and then. Pat was top dog. There was a gate across a draw that was in plain sight of the house. Anyone coming by car had to stop and open the gate. Old Pat had a real rough bark, and he would run down towards the gate. Most people would hurry to get through, shut the gate, and try to be back in the car before Pat got there. There was nothing to worry about tho', Pat's bark was worse than his bite and he never bit anyone that I ever knew of. However, they did tell a story about when Pat was a young dog. Sheep outfits used to trail a mile east of Johnsons. Someone lost a lamb and someone else brought it over to the Johnsons. That lamb and Pat played all summer until one day towards fall while nobody was home, Pat apparently decided that that lamb had grown into a sheep and killed it. Pat was the first dog that I worked, and was a good working dog. I used him to pull the sled when I went to pick up mail. The sled I used was home-made out of skis with a box, 2 feet by 3 feet, 8 or 10 inches above the skis. We would leave the ski ends stuck in the snow and stand the sled up too. After lunch if I came out and laid the sled down, Pat would be beside himself. He knew that we were going down country for the mail and he could hardly stand still

Pat the police dog moving his new dog house.

until I got him harnessed and away he'd go. I'd get on my skis and probably not catch up with him for half a mile. We never followed the snow trail.

The boys told of one time Pop was out on the feed trail and sneezed and lost his false teeth in the snow. The boys went to help find them and took the garden rake and looked and looked but did not find them and gave up. Old Pat the dog was along and Del got to playing with the dog by making snowballs for Pat to catch. Lo and behold that dog picked up the teeth with one of those snowballs!

It was customary to raise dogs around a fox farm. Wayne Light raised Great Danes around his fox farm in Steamboat Springs. One time when the depression was at its worst, Wayne had a dog to sell. He had been getting $100 and up for each, but he priced this dog at $75 and was not having any luck selling. When Frank Light, his father, came back from wintering in the south, he told Wayne, "People are afraid there is something wrong with that dog." So the price went back up and they sold the dog. Johnsons, to my knowledge, never got that kind of price for any of the police dogs that they raised.

There was a litter born one fall. They were kept inside of the fox farm which had an 8-foot board fence around it. They got rid of all the pups but one. By the time he got out and about, we were snowed in. That winter Del and I decided to try tanning some hides and furs. We had gotten hold of some chrome tan chemicals that required wood containers which we did not have. Del knew of a small barrel that was up at Ed Gamber's cabin. Del wanted to know if I would go get it and I said, "Sure." I hitched up Pat to the sled and started out with this pup following along. Pat was a big dog and stayed fat, whereas Mike, the pup, weighed very little and had big feet. Mike would walk on the snow that Pat broke through continually. We had not gone a mile when I had the bright idea of switching dogs. Mike had no problem pulling the sled, and Pat was ready to call it a day and return home.

I had a successful trip and retrieved the barrel. The only trouble was, Mike had never been worked before and his shoulders were not toughened up, so they got sore. Mike never worked good again and would balk or run away. When spring came and cars started running, it was a sight to see that big ole pup Mike run and hide in the willows the first time he saw a car.

One spring when I was setting out beaver traps, I had Pat pulling the sled hauling the traps for me. I was on skis and there were still snow banks on the beaver dams as I worked down the creek. Most places there was still a couple feet of snow that dropped right off into the water. Pat would stay on one side of the creek and if I happened to be on the other side I'd call to Pat and he would follow along. This one time I started skiing down and hollered, "Come on, Pat!" I heard a splash. He had jumped into the creek, sled, traps, and all! I was able to find a place where I could reach and get hold of the harness and pull him out without losing any traps.

The Johnson brothers, Del and Curley, had a sawmill for years. They cut most of their logs on the Forest and had to have timber marked with a U.S. stamp because the ranger picked the trees that they were to harvest. I think stumpage was $2 a thousand in the 30's. Dry stuff for house logs and firewood was

The Johnson sawmill. Del sawing and Pop supervising.

free. Rough lumber sold for around $20 a thousand, some more and some less.

The mill itself was a steam driven mill, sort of put together. There was a Case boiler, a Reeves two-cylinder engine, and parts of several different steam engines. The Reeves engine was set up along the side of the Case boiler. It ran and sawed lumber. Some times they cut firewood to fire the boiler, other times they cut up slabs. One thing for sure you did *not* take Maw Johnson any slabs to cook with, nothing but number one dry solid wood. Not only was the cooking done with wood, all heating was done by wood too. That included the fox shop, the bunkhouse, as well as the main house. There was a steam-powered cutoff saw they used to cut all the firewood into stove or boiler lengths. Water for the boiler was sucked up from a small stream that ran close by, or they would put a tank on a bobsled and haul water from a spring. They did both. Maybe the stream was not always sufficient, but it was a lot handier putting the injection pipe in a stream than having to haul water and drain everything at night.

Much of the lumber that was being sawed in 1933-1934 was for the new house that was started. It was being built of 6-inch logs, sawed three sides, with a bark face. These logs had to be planed to be the same size, as did the 1x4 that was laid between the logs. There could be no variation in thickness or the dovetail corners would be off. After the logs were laid up, the space in front of the 1x4 was daubed with a special cement. That was a big house, a long way around, and there were not many days that Del laid one complete round of logs.

They sawed all the flooring, the dimension lumber for everything that went into the house, and the shingles too. The barn was already built in 1933, built of logs with dovetailed corners. Those corners were Del Johnson's trademark. I never saw anyone else make dovetailed corners but there were buildings with them that had been built before. Delmer used an adz to cut them out and had homemade gages to tell how deep to cut each face.

I did help work on the house, mostly helping to get the logs up when it got a ways up. Also I helped at the sawmill by firing the boiler. That is where I learned the difference in firewood that Maw knew all along.

Another duty when firing the boiler was to keep the water level up which was done by a steam operated injector. It was only a matter of turning a valve or two to get the water level right in the water glass and there was a blower in the front of the flues that increased the draft when more steam was needed. Firing that boiler was where I learned to leave a chimney, you couldn't keep the steam pressure up unless the flames could get up through the wood, we would split the bigger blocks to make a chimney. Slabs had to be crossed to make a chimney.

Right here I better admit I never saw a sharp ax, or saw until I went to North Park! At home about the only thing to saw or chop was used railroad ties that were full of gravel-filled cracks.

In 1933 there were no chain saws! Trees were felled with about a 6-foot crosscut saw with a handle on each end. Then they were cut into saw log lengths and skidded to the log pile by a horse named Maude. There was a skidway built consisting of logs sloped up as high as a wagon so that the saw logs could be rolled up to load a wagon or sled as the case may have been.

Trapping was how I was to try to make wages in winter. I had trapped some on dry land, mostly coyotes and badgers. Water trapping was all new to me. There were plenty of traps of all sizes from 0 to a bear trap, 0 traps were used mostly for weasel (ermine) and same for muskrats. Size 1 worked better for muskrats, what I called "rats." Size 1½ were used for mink and martin. Size 3's and 4's were used to catch beaver, badger, coyotes, and fox. Bear traps were size 12 or 14's.

The first fur I went after in the fall was muskrats, because there was such a short time before the creeks froze over. North Park rats were not especially good or big because they were under the ice for half of the year. I also set out a couple of mink sets. I used mink boxes that were about 3 feet long made of 10 inch lumber. These had 4 sides and no ends until it got to freezing. Then you put one end to the edge of the water and the other end in a trail in the grass. The trap on land was covered with grass or leaves, whatever looked natural, the trap at the other end was put in the water. The muskrat traps were put where the water was deep enough for the rat to drown, as were the beaver traps, otherwise sometimes they could twist a front leg off and be gone. I always ran the rat traps first thing in the morning.

That first year I did not trap beaver in the fall, because fall beaver were not as prime as spring beaver. The State of Colorado demanded half of all beavers caught and skinned. This is the way it was done: after you had caught, skinned, and stretched the pelts you sent them into the State. They would market them and send you half of the money or they would tag half and send them back to you. You could sell a tagged beaver, but it was illegal to sell an untagged one.

I started trapping about the first week in October. By the middle of October I would start setting coyote and badger traps. After the snow got to accumulating, it was the time to set traps where the wind would keep it blown bare. To begin with, I would set 10 or 12 sets. After it got to snowing, I would cut those down to 6 or 8 sets. Then around my birthday (Nov 5th) I would set the weasel line. It ran from the road out south on the east side of the creek, up around past Ed Gamber's cabin, east to Doran creek, down thru the Doran place and home, 8 or 9 miles. Then there was a shorter line north that was run another day. These traps were put out horseback and run horseback until the snow got too deep. That is when I learned to ski. There must have been more than 50 weasel boxes, same as mink boxes but half as long, an 0 trap fastened in each end. They were located at fence brace corners and under willow bushes that stood out sort of alone along the creeks. Most were already in place and after I had learned where to look I was able to find most of them. At first I used pieces of rabbit for bait. I'd put the bait in the middle and set a trap in each end. No cover was needed as they would jump right into an uncovered trap. Weasels are cannibals and it turned out that weasel carcass made the best bait.

As the snow got deeper, the box was lifted up and set on top of the snow. A weasel has a keen sense of smell. Even when the box was covered, a weasel would dive down and go through the box. I might explain that the ground very seldom froze under that much snow. Therefore mice and moles lived under the snow and they were the staple food for weasels. They would travel on top of the snow until it had snowed to a certain depth, then under the snow they would go to spend the rest of the winter. As I recall, the depth was between 3 and 4 feet, when weasel trapping would come to an end.

I have neglected to point out that weasels are brown until the snow comes, then they turn white and become known as ermine. I probably caught more ermine than any other fur.

Thirteen were the most that I ever caught in one day. They averaged about 45¢ to 50¢ each. Muskrats were always a little cheaper than ermine, probably a dime cheaper. Coyotes averaged in the neighborhood of $5 to $7. Badgers and mink were about the same or a little higher. Martin was the prize catch and would bring about $18. Some red fox brought near that, but they generally averaged around $12 to $14. That brings us to beaver. They probably averaged $7 to $8 if they were tagged. And that was for half of what you had skinned and stretched. The State Of Colorado took their half. I'll admit this: some I shared with Colorado, some I bootlegged. Remember we had just ended Prohibition and knew what bootlegging was all about. I did trap some beaver later that spring tho' that I dutifully shared with the State of Colorado.

We tanned several beaver hides, mostly kits, or young beaver, because they had thinner, lighter hides that tanned and worked up nicer than older beaver. But the kits had very little value. Maw Johnson made me a pair of mittens out of beaver one winter that were great. She put the fur inside and left the cuffs untrimmed so there was a nice fur cuff that when turned down made the best nose-wiper ever. The beaver hide wore very well. In fact I wore those mittens until the fur wore out of the palms and they were no longer warm.

When the Johnsons came to North Park in 1914 there was a bear pen already built up in Bear Park. I do not recall who showed it to Del, but he had caught some 20 bear in the same spot where I set the bear trap in the spring of 1934. A bear pen consisted of a V-shaped pen built by fastening a cover around two sides of a triangular formation of trees. The trap was set in the open side with the bait put in the middle. Bear traps were size 12's or 14's and had to be set with clamps, one to each spring. The clamps were hung within reach of the trap so if someone happened to get caught they could get free.

I got a piece of horse meat from the fox farm for bait and skied up, set the trap, and caught a yearling brown bear number

21 in that same location. I do not recall what I ever did with that bear hide.

Del told of two things that were there when they settled there. One was Ptarmigan that had been quite plentiful. They were not around the buildings while I was there, although there were a nice group at the head of Big Park that I saw each summer.

Lynx cats had also been quite plentiful in the early years and Del had caught many of them. I never saw one but I did find a pair of tracks one spring near Bennett Lake when there was about an inch of new snow. I followed those tracks up past Bear Park until the new snow melted but I never got sight of him. Those were the only Lynx tracks I ever saw. Deer tho', were another story. Deer were much more plentiful in 1933 than they had been in 1914.

Feeding was my responsibility. It took a sled load of hay a day to feed Otto's 35 to 50 head of cattle and their calves. This is the procedure that we followed. We would get a load of hay on the sled, pull it around to head out of the round corral, and hitch up the team. Pop would get up on the hay, pull his hat down good, and take a fresh grip on his pipe as I opened the gate. The team would turn slightly, break the front runners loose, and be off on a dead run. Sometimes he would get them stopped by the time they got to the barn, or he would have to make a circle and come back to pick me up. Then we would go and feed the cows and the calves in separate bunches. We would come back to the barn and clean it. We kept the team and a couple of milk cows in nights with lots of bedding. I would use a wheelbarrow and wheel the old bedding out over a plank that we ran out of the barn. We would take this bedding and feed the fox horses who were winterin' along the feed trail. By spring when the surrounding snow melted and one got up on the hill east and looked down, it looked like a giant serpent, as it wound across the meadow. The accumulated manure insulated the trail, and kept it from melting as fast.

How we broke trail to a new stack.

The first thing I learned about feed trails was to go to the farther stack first. As you fed it out then there was a trail near the other stacks, as you worked back towards home. We always drug a plank behind the back bobs to level the snow. If the snow wasn't leveled it would build up to a peak and you couldn't keep a sled on it.

There were all kinds of feed horses, but the best ones came from where the snow got deep like at Johnsons because those horses knew how to follow a trail, any mark in the snow! Pop had a team of little mares that we used as a lead team that were the best I ever saw at following a feed trail. There could be a foot of new snow and everything look the same, we would start out and they would hit a trot but never step off the trail. If you got stuck they would balk. If the trail was good we would use just one team but if there was new snow or the trail was bad, like it could be in the spring, then we'd use four horses.

Earlier that year during haying Otto Johnson and I broke three geldings–a black, a bay, and a grey. We used those broncs to feed with that first winter. They weren't named, so I named them Tom, Dick, and Harry. Tom, the black one, turned out to be what we called an outlaw. Tom kicked Pop out of the stall one morning while he was being harnessed. He kicked me while I was unhitching one day, and he kicked Del once. In fact, he was never to be trusted as long as he lived, but he never refused to pull and never gave out...along with his cussedness.

One thing I can say, the disposition of all horses has improved considerable in my lifetime, there are not near the knotheads or outlaws that there were when I grew up.

Pop Johnson did not have a work bridle in the place with blinds. He said that he'd seen more runaways when a horse rubbed a bridle off with blinds than any other cause of runaways. But that didn't mean they wouldn't run when they had a mind to anyway!

One time we were opening a new crib just after it had snowed and there must have been close to two feet of loose snow. We had just one team, Tom and Dick, and they were goosey. We pulled up along side of the stack, the crib was 8 feet tall, with the haystack piled on that. The procedure was that I'd get up on the back of the hayrack with 2 pitchforks, stick one in the hay, climb up, and stick the other one higher until I got on top. Then Pop would throw the scoop shovel up and I'd shovel the snow off. In the meantime Pop made a turnaround beyond the stack and waited until I got the snow off. The fox horses had followed our trail in towards the stack. When Pop pulled alongside the stack, the team decided that was a good time to pull a runaway and away they went down the trail. Most of the loose horses got out of the way, but one old mare tried to outrun them and got overtook. Tom went on one side and Dick the other. She was in 2 feet of loose snow and got run over, team, sled, and all. After they cleared her, she laid stretched out in the snow. I thought, "There is another horse to butcher." After a moment she rolled her eyes, jumped up, and had a runaway all of her own. She ran clear to the far side of the field before she looked back to see if anything was following.

Pop and I worked some of those fox horses toward spring to have something to do. None of them turned out to be good enough to keep.

Pop Johnson used to pull down his hat a lot. I'll explain. There were two old timers that wore a skull cap underneath their hat in the winter. Pop was one, and the other was old Louie from over on Pony Creek. Old Lou was the only one I ever talked to who had come up the trail from Texas. Skull caps were made from the top of a woman's stocking using the reinforced part cut off with a string tied around it.

Lou told me he for sure never rode point or even swing on the trail herd. He said, "I was in the drag and dust, with the lame and crippled ones." He couldn't recall where they started from, but he told me when they got to Lamar, Colorado, his trailing days ended. Lou fancied himself as some sort of a gunslinger. He practiced quick draw and had a number of cap and ball pistols he molded the bullets for out of lead. He use to shoot into a quaker block and when he ran short of bullets he would split the block, retrieve the bullets, and cast them over. He was not what you would call a top cow hand.

Back to the Johnsons, they had a model-T Ford coupe. Del and I went to Steamboat in it the first fall to get cereal for the fox rations. "Cereal" consisted of sweepings from the Post Toasties factory that we got from Wayne Light. When coming back over Rabbit Ears Pass that Ford heated up. Del had a bucket along and he knew where every source of water was along the way. When we would stop, I would drain the radiator. Del would take the bucket, leave, and return with a cold bucket of Rocky Mountain spring water. We probably changed water three times coming up the west side of Rabbit Ears Pass that day.

One winter a man by the name of Harold Emigh stayed a few days at Johnsons. Harold had built a snow plane and he let me have a ride. A snow plane is a kind of a wingless airplane that runs on skis. Let me tell you, I was *real* impressed at moving across the snow at such a speed!

Harold Emigh's snow plane at Johnsons 1934.

I had been running the weasel line horseback and when the snow got deeper and it got harder for a horse to get around this dry-lander tackled skis. There was a pair of maple skis at Johnsons that I used. They were lighter than hickory skis, 7-feet long, and equipped with a toe strap and binders made of leather straps that buckled to fit with a strap over the instep to keep the strap from falling down. There were no ski boots. At least I had none. I used overshoes worn over felt shoes. That was equipment in 1933 in North Park. Poles were bamboo or cane with a cane basket fastened with leather and a steel point. That is what I started skiing with. I practiced skiing three times. When I went out the 4th time I tackled the weasel line–all 9 miles of it. By the time I got to the sled trail a mile or so east of the house, I took those skis off and carried them home, one tired boy! From then on tho' I ran the weasel line on skis and after I got used to it I skied a martin line up in the timber on the Forest.

There was a ridge west up on the forest that had an old timber road to the top. Towards spring I'd climb up there on skis. The trip would take most of an hour going up and maybe 5 minutes home.

The Turner kids skied too. They were in school in Walden

and skied home weekends. That was the extent of skiing in the neighborhood in 1933.

Later tho', around 1935 or '36, some of the ranchers on the west side began to get together for Sunday ski parties. After the feeding was done they would load the family on a bobsled along with the makings of a potluck dinner and meet the neighbors for lunch and an afternoon of skiing. They would leave in time for all to get home for the evening chores. On occasion, a rancher would take a four horse team and pick up neighbors as they went and pull skiers behind. It was up to everyone to get uphill on their own, and there was a toboggan for those who didn't ski.

These ski parties surely led to the first ski tow, which was built by Delmer Johnson and put into operation in the fall of 1937 at the Johnson ranch in Crosby Draw. Delmer used a wooden wagon wheel that was grooved for the rope to run in. This was mounted on a horse-drawn mowing machine frame and powered by an air-cooled gas engine from Monkey Wards. Also ordered from Monkeys was a thousand feet of $5/8$- or $3/8$-inch hemp rope. As I recall we had less than a hundred feet of rope left after going uphill, around the pulley, back downhill and around the wagon wheel, and spliced. We knew that if the rope got wet it wouldn't last, so we got roofing tar and covered it completely. You could always tell if anyone had been skiing at Johnsons by the tar on the mitts and jackets!

From that time on ski tows multiplied and eventually skiing became the industry it is today. Cross-country skiing has mostly gone out of style and ranchers today use snowmobiles to get around in snow...a far cry from when I started in 1933!

Along in spring I met Pete Maroney. Pete Maroney was a character in North Park by anybody's standards. He lived in Coalmont and spent most of the summers fishing and hauling dudes to the high country in a wagon made of the chassis of model T Ford and pulled by a team of horses. So Pete would fish, and when hunting season came he did that too.

The Johnson ski tow.

I did take a drink with Pete Maroney one time in hunting season. He and some hunters were camped on top between Round Mountain and Mad Creek. I rode into camp and they offered me a drink. No, they offered me a bottle that I could drink from. The weather was cold and so was I, so I drank after Pete Maroney with, surprisingly, no bad effects.

One time I was coming down Buffalo Pass road and it started to rain like it never does except in haying time. I got my slicker on and as I came around a curve lo and behold here comes this dude in shirt sleeves with his hat on the back of his head and drunker than a skunk. I asked, "Where are you going?" He slurred, "Just for a little walk. It's a hell of a nice day fer a little walk." About then Pete came around into sight with several more in the same shape in his wagon.

I fished in Round Mt. Lake one day and cleaned the fish before I left. In a day or two I went to use my pocket knife, and realized I had left it at Round Mt. Lake. It was several days before I got back that way. When I did I saw where Pete had camped on top and rode his horse down to the lake. When I got there my knife was gone. Later I met Pete and asked him if he

BILL CULBERTSON
© 1994

found my knife. He said, "Yes." And that was that. He never gave it back to me, or said thanks.

Pete used to leave his saddle horse on the forest with a bell on him when he went home. That horse never went too far from the Ranger Station and one day I ran across Pete's horse. When I saw that bell I tossed a loop on him and relieved him of the bell and neck strap. I thought that would be a fair trade for my knife! I hid the bell and got to Manvilles and told Al about it and why I had done it. He said, "Don't bring that bell here, Pete may go on the prod!" I eventually took it to Johnsons and it was still there when I went off to the war.

Pete Maroney was a tough old Irishman tho' and he would get on horses that younger men wouldn't and ride them. He reminded me of Tex Jacques, the last of the wolf trappers in the area. Tex was around Johnsons for a couple of years and when he was there he would tell me about some of his experiences. I always took them with a grain of salt but after Tex was dead and gone I was talking to the local doctor one day and Tex's name came up. I said "Tex was a bag of wind!" Doc asked if I had ever seen him with his clothes off and I said "No." He said that Tex had knife scars and bullet holes from one end to the other. Just goes to show I may have known some tough hombres in my time.

We became aware of Rocky Mountain Spotted Fever, in the early 30's when it broke out in the Bitter Root Valley of Montana. It was caused by wood ticks biting people when the ticks first came out in the spring. Several deaths were reported and that got our attention.

One spring I was helping Turpens build fence across sage brush country. Lou Krause, another young lad, and I were the crew. Every evening when we got into the bunk house we would strip and hunt for ticks. Us young ones would find a tick or two, Lou would find a dozen! We never told Lou, but we figured those ticks were hatching out of his old undershirt.

I had tick fever one spring. I had a tick bite me while I was trapping beaver and several days later while running my traps,

I got sick. I finally got to the house and kept getting worse. That evening Del went to Coalmont and got the new coal company doctor. Dr. Morgan was young and new, and he gave some pills that broke my fever by midnight. It took me about a week to recover.

On St. Patricks Day in 1934 I was over in the Doran picking up some traps on skis. It rained enough to soften the snow in the sage brush until it would not hold me and that made for a rough trip home.

The winter of 1933 and 1934 turned out to be a light snow winter with less than 4 feet of snow at the house. It also was to be one of the shortest snow winters in North Park up to then. The road opened up in April and Cecil Harrington, who had a homestead in Clover Valley and serviced radios, came in his old Chevy to Johnsons and stayed a day or two. He mentioned that he was going to The Big Horn cow camp at Lake Creek. Pop Johnson suggested that I go over and see about a job which I did. I was hired by Fred Egry, the cow foreman, to work on the corrals at Lake Creek because The Big Horn as well as all of North Park had to dip for scabies that year. Later I was to ride for the Big Horn cow outfit.

I gathered my clothes and bedroll and borrowed a saddle from Curley Johnson. My own saddle was at home on the dry land. Pop Johnson gave me $20 for overall money as promised and I had made a little over $30 a month from trapping. I left satisfied. I had lived a life different from how I was raised and enjoyed it immensely.

As I gathered up my gear and headed for The Big Horn, I was about to experience yet another way of making a living.

I had quite some experience in disturbing cattle while growing up. We always had cattle as well as milk cows. We also ran a day herd. I had worked for other people handling cattle and had rode horses since I was very young and now here I was joining a cow outfit as a *FULL-TIME COWBOY*!

"The Big Horn bunkhouses have all the conveniences of a modern jail!"

—*Bill Angel, c1934*

A Big Horn Cowboy

This bit of information is offered as a general account of the Big Horn of North Park during the time that I was involved there from 1934 to 1950. This account also includes some of the people there before my time.

All dates may not be correct but I've done my best and apologize for any errors that I have made.

Charles Boettcher came to North Park in 1882 from Leadville, Colorado, where he had been in the hardware and mercantile business. He had several partners including N.L. Jones. In fact the brand ⩔ was recorded to Jones and Boettcher in the first Colorado Brand Book in 1885. Mr. Boettcher filed on a homestead on the west side of what is now known as Lake Boettcher or Lake Creek.

The grand plan was to raise horses to pull the streetcars in Denver. By the time they got their horse herd built up, the streetcars in Denver were being moved be electricity. The early horse herd was in the charge of Ken McCallum.

In 1884 Mr. Boettcher requested his brother-in-law, John W. Riggen, to come to Lake Creek and look it over. Riggen liked what he saw, went back to Kansas, sold his farm, and moved his family to Lake Creek in 1885. John then became the first manager of what was to be The Big Horn.

Some of the improvements made while Mr. Riggen was manager from 1885 to 1894 include the digging of the Little Nelly Ditch, constructing the 30 foot high irrigation flume across the Gap, ditching the big meadow in squares (as can be seen today), and increasing both the cattle and horse herds.

In 1891 when the house at Lake Creek burned down the Riggen family moved to what was to become known as the Boettcher Ranch. It is presumed that Mr. Boettcher left North Park some time after the Riggen family came.

There were five children in the Riggen family, so when it came time for school and high school Mrs. Riggen moved to Walden during the school term. In 1894 Riggens moved to a ranch that they had bought near Walden and Charles Riggen, the oldest son, took over as manager of The Big Horn, altho John Riggen remained active in ventures like The Big Horn Mining, Ditch and Land Company, which was incorporated in September 1896. This was the first use of The Big Horn name by the Boettchers.

The Big Horn Mining, Ditch and Land Company constructed the dam in Big Creek Lake, dug the ditch to Trotman Draw, installed the inverted flume across Trotman Draw, and dug the Ditch around Independence Mountain to Placer Draw where they did considerable Placer Gold Mining starting in 1898 and ending in 1900 when they were unable to hold the ditch on the steep side of Independence Mountain.

The Big Horn Post Office was in section 35, Township 11 North, range 81 West, where the Placer camp was from March 3rd, 1898, to February 5th, 1900, with John W. Riggen also serving as the only postmaster.

Late in 1902 Mr. Boettcher decided to change managers, replacing Charles Riggen with Mr. William Marr of Hebron. Mr. Boettcher wrote letters to both but put the letters in the wrong envelopes, sending the Marr letter to Riggen and the Riggen letter to Marr. I understand that caused quite a lot of hard feelings, but the change did take place.

Also in 1902, The Big Horn Land and Cattle Company was formed, with Mr. Marr putting in his ranch known as The Big Horn Ranch that included the Home Ranch, the School Section Ranch, and Clover Valley along with other lands, the cattle, the cattle brand =M, horses, and the horse brand ∃.

The first board of directors of The Big Horn Land and Cattle Company were Charles Boettcher, William Marr, William Boyd Page, John F. Campion, and J. Carrol Back.

Added in 1906 was the Hill Ranch and later the Shafer Ranch. Among the homesteads added were the Herb Hill (the upper and lower), the DeWeese and the Mansfield to name a few. In 1928 the Hanson Ranch was added and in the 40's the Hunter Ranch was bought.

Ranches leased through the years were the Staples, the Norris, the Keoughan, the Rosenbaum, and the Coolidge Ranch as well as many acres of deeded pasture land.

When The Big Horn was started, everything that was not fenced was free range! The National Forest was created by an act of Congress in 1891, but it was 1904 before it was funded, and Forest Rangers started permitting livestock grazing and charging a fee.

The Winter of 1909 was a long, hard winter which caused a shortage of hay in all of North Park. The Big Horn was no exception.

Billy McGowan was cow foreman at the time and he later told me about The Big Horn cowboys taking the horse herd to the Laramie Plains where there was plenty of grass.

They came back to the Park and started back out with some 1,500 cows. Stephen Paine mentioned in the book *Where the Rockies Ride Herd*, how The Big Horn went by the Paine place in the night. They never stopped day or night. They were probably on the trail for three days, but if Billy told me I've forgotten. There was a team and sled along to try to rustle up some grub. I don't know how that worked either, but Billy told of how he'd tell the rest of them, "Wait until we get to where we can see the Laramie Plains, there will be grass as far as we can see!" When they got to where the Laramie Plains could be seen...WHITE! It had snowed two feet while they were gone.

All they could do was turn the cattle loose up the Laramie River, where there was some brush showing, but not enough to sustain a cow. Billy McGowan and another cowboy stayed and as the cows calved they gave the new born calves to anyone who would take them. Mostly they killed the calves as they were born tho' to try to save the cows. Billy told of a small stack of hay that was on the ranch they were staying at. He said he would fill a gunnysack with hay and give some to some poor cow when he'd have to shoot her calf. He said that by spring he had carried off most of that haystack in a gunnysack.

It was reported that The Big Horn branded some 400 calves in the Spring of 1909 where they had been branding 1,500 calves before.

Billy McGowan was the first cow foreman that I heard of. Then there was Albert Manville, Fred McKinzie, Fred Egry (who hired me), and Frank Hoskinson. There were several more during WWII. When I came back and was there from 1946 thru 1950 Duane Hagler was the foreman.

We have covered the managers John W. Riggen and Charles Riggen which brings us to William Marr, who managed until his death in 1916. William's brother A.K. Marr then returned from Denver and managed The Big Horn until he too died about 1920. Then is when Mr. Boettcher hired John F. "Jack" White, who managed The Big Horn until after the south end sold in 1941. W.A. Simson (Blunt), managed the north end until he had a heart attack, during WWII. Waldo Axelson managed during the years that C.J. Ryan owned The Big Horn from 1946-1950. Jack Ferguson managed for Davis and McIlvaine, followed by Carl Hanson then Cebe Hanson who manages now.

A note of interest, as long as the Boettchers or Mr. Ryan owned The Big Horn there were no tractors on, or owned by, The Big Horn. When Ryan sold to the Vogler Group in 1950 the

BILL CULBERTSON
© 1994

only gasoline equipment was two light plants and one old pickup. There were some 2,100 cows, 80 bulls, and 365 horses went with that deal.

Some of the Boettcher family owned a Denver bank, when that bank foreclosed on a Wyoming sheep outfit in 1928, some

10,000 sheep, herders, dogs, and the works were shipped to Cowdrey. The Big Horn was then in the sheep business until 1941 when Mr. Boettcher sold The South End which consisted of the Home Ranch, the School Section Ranch, and Clover Valley. He also gave up leases on the School House flats, and the Coalmont flats, plus thousands of acres of pasture land including Forest Permits and Taylor Grazing Permits that had been free range.

The North End was the Boettcher Ranch, Shafer Ranch, Hill Ranch, Lake Creek Ranch, and the Hanson Ranch. Later the Hunter Ranch was acquired.

In 1931 Jack White changed the operation of The Big Horn Ranches. Except for the Hanson ranch, the company had been paying all wages to the ranch foremen and all help. Mr. White put the ranch foremen on contract! They were to furnish all labor to irrigate, hay and fence stacks for $2 a ton, then get 50¢ a ton for feeding the hay out. There was a clause that said, "The Big Horn will pay 33¢ a meal or $1 a day for meals fed to the cow outfit."

When I started riding for The Big Horn I got to know all the ranch managers fairly quickly. On the Boettcher Ranch was W.A. "Blunt" Simson, on the Shafer was John Ugalo, on the Hill Ranch and Lake Creek was Horace Mason, on the Home Ranch was Charlie Freeman, on the School Section, Dewy Norell, and on the MacFarlane (Keoughan) was Frank Montgomery until he left that fall and was replaced by Billy McGowan who came and stayed until 1941. On the Curtis Place, by the MacFarlane Reservoir, was Roy Noe, and on the Hanson Ranch was Jack White, his wife Ann, sons Forman and Bill, and Waldo Axelson as ranch foreman.

The Wamsley Brothers, Burl and Walt contracted the School House flats and the Coalmont flats.

For what it's worth Charlie Shell wrote some notes about being ranch foreman on the Home Ranch from 1922 to 1932. In 1923 he reports that The Big Horn was running 5,200 cattle,

325 bulls and 2,100 horses. They were paying taxes on 93,000 acres and leasing around 100,000 acres throughout North Park.

Hay production reported in the 1920's at the Home Ranch. The hay crop ran from 1,100 to 1,500 tons, the School Section ran from 1,100 to 1,200 tons, the Boettcher Ranch ran from 3,800 to 4,000 tons, the Shafer Ranch from 900 tons to 1,100 tons, the Hill Ranch from 1,200 to 1,500 tons, Lake Creek Ranch from 800 to 900 tons, and the MacFarlane Ranch which produced from 1,600 to 1,800 tons. Leased was what was known as the Coolidge Ranch that put up from 1,500 to 1,800 tons.

It is also noted that The Big Horn bought from 3,000 to 3,500 tons of hay yearly and in the winter a man would be paid 75¢ a ton for feeding the hay out. They would give him 500 cows to feed.

Some habits and customs on The Big Horn in the 30's. Cow outfit wages were $40 a month signed by a Miss Toogood, a secretary in the Denver office who I never met.

When I went to work for The Big Horn cow outfit about April 20th, 1934, the outfit consisted of Fred Egry, the cow foreman, Bert Wilcox, Bill Angel, Frank Hoskinson, Hank McDaniels, and me, the kid of the outfit. I received $30 a month. The wage for the rest was $40 a month, the highest ranch pay in North Park then. But after 1934 whenever I rode for them I too got $40 a month, up to 1941.

At Lake Creek Fred Egry lived in the house, his wife Lois, who had just had twins, was elsewhere. Herb Brownlee, who was trapping beaver over on the North Fork, was staying in the bunkhouse. On the Boettcher and Shafer ranches, the other cowboys came and went.

I do recall one time when they were all there, they got to talking about roping different wild animals. Several had roped coyotes, one had been along when a wolf had been roped, one had roped an elk, and a couple had roped a bear, but they all agreed that a wild horse gave you more fight than any of these others.

*Frank Hoskinson at
Lake Creek in 1934.*

Frank Hoskinson was a rangy character with a protruding lower lip. One day I asked about it. Seems he had a so-so saddle horse that got out with the wild horses on the west slope, he was on his best saddle horse trying to get this horse back in. He said "I had a wreck–a bad one. They had to gather me up with a wagon!" He went on to say that there had been a hell of a lot more good horses ruined or killed running wild horses than good horses caught.

Frank had quite a few stories. One he used to like to tell was about the time he brought a 4-horse team with a sled-load of people to a hotel in Steamboat Springs for a ski tournament. They were drinking and talking when someone among them wondered how it would feel to come off the BIG ski jump. Frank said he wouldn't be afraid to come off it and ended up betting the price of the hotel bill for the group that he would come off it. He said "I borrowed a pair of skis and climbed to the to. Only problem was, I got about half sober by the time I got there, but I put the skis on and headed down. I had a great big wreck, but I lived and didn't have to pay the hotel bill!"

Frank had a place of his own on the west slope. He told about a horse roundup at his place. When they got the roundup corralled Frank went into his cabin and got lunch. When the other 4 men came in they told Frank, "When we got the horses worked we had just 4 unbranded horses, so we each branded one." Frank said he picked up the pot of stew and headed for the door. Right quick they wanted to know where he was going. He said, "I'm going to throw this out! I'll not feed you while you steal a horse from me!" They thawed quick, one gave him a bill of sale for his horse, another gave him $10, and another gave him half interest in his horse. Then they ate the stew.

Frank also told of a bunch of elk being planted near his place. He noticed the elk coming out of the willows of an evening and one day he got on a horse and slipped between them and the willows. When the elk ran across the meadow he said "I ran up on them quick, their heads looked like a bucket hung on a stick so I jerked my rope down, roped a cow, busted her, and broke her neck." Somebody was going by, saw the performance, and turned him in. He said, "They fined me $500 and I thought for awhile they were going to hang me besides!"

The bunkhouse at Lake Creek was built of hand squared logs made with a broad ax and dovetail corners. It was a single room, and had been the office at the Big Horn Placer Mine in Placer Draw when it was operating from 1898 to 1900. Very likely it was the post office too. I noticed several strands of barb wire twisted together that came down from the attic and were stapled to the logs for a couple of feet. I wondered about that until one day the wind blew...

My Saturday night entertainment at the Lake Creek cow camp.

The buildings are on the east side of the Hog Back. The prevailing wind was from the southwest, therefore the wind that came through Ute Pass was headed right for Lake Creek. I had been raised on the dry lands and thought I'd seen some wind until I stayed at Lake Creek! There were whirlwinds that would take water near a hundred feet in the air. Besides strong winds blowing down the Hog Back there were strong winds that blew up the Hog Back. There had been a calf shed built there several years before it had been blown UP the hill several hundred feet.

There were lots of coots then, and I use to wonder if they dived down to the bottom of the lake and grabbed a rock in each paddle-foot when the wind hit.

There is a gap in the Hog Back a mile or so south of the Lake Creek buildings, that is notorious for strong winds. There's a story that some of The Big Horn cowboys had been sampling some moonshine and were riding west through the gap when the wind quit and one cowboy fell off over his horse's head.

Another time Frank Hoskinson got his Model A Ford stuck in the snow in the gap and finally gave up and walked to the

Boettcher Ranch for the night. The wind came up and blew all the snow away except what was under the four tires, there sat his car near two feet off the ground! After learning about the winds at Lake Creek, I knew that those strands of barb wire were to hold the lid on the bunkhouse!

When I started working I worked alone. I was given a team and a wagon running gears and told where to go. It turned out to be the old Lee Conrad homestead south of the Shafer Ranch. There was a nice stand of pine and I cut posts for the Lake Creek corrals. After I had cut several loads, I was told to dig post holes across one corral to divide it. I dug the holes and never looked back until I got to the other side. Well, they were crooked. So I did considerable more digging before they would line up.

I suppose that Fred Egry did the cooking until one day he brought Lindsey Coe and Earl Boston out to work on the corrals. A few days later Egry went up Mexican Creek, for, of all things, some moonshine. There was a woman lived up Mexican Creek that had a homestead, a still, and a live-in man. I do not recall the moonshine, but Egry hired the man. We needed a cook and Red Snyder, an old roundup cook, joined us. To say the least we were an interesting group. From those days on I heard many a tale by Lindsey Coe. I never got tired of his tales and humor. Lindsey had been cow foreman for the Big Creek outfit, a moonshiner, a bootlegger, and a gambler just to name a few. This was the crew that I left with when I started riding for The Big Horn cow outfit on May 2nd, 1934.

That first day we were to move 1,700 yearlings from the Boettcher Ranch to the Home Ranch, by Hebron, to start dipping for scabies. On this trip were Hank McDaniels, Frank Hoskinson, Bill Angel, and me. They gave me an old horse by the name of Sage. As we saddled up I had to change the cinch to fit Sage which delayed me some. The others got saddled up, rode off and left me. When I got saddled up and mounted, I put the spurs to old Sage, but he didn't take to being hurried and bucked for a while before we agreed to get along. I did catch up and I'm sure the others didn't miss anything even if they were riding away from the action. Just after we got through the Gap we ran across a mare that had laid down next to a puddle and had a colt into the water. We got it out but too late. The brand on the mare was the key and told us she belonged to the Brands.

The way that we moved cattle on The Big Horn was that someone took the lead and someone else took the drag. On this day Frank Hoskinson and Hank McDaniels took the lead. That left Bill Angel and me in the drag. Away we went, around Sheep Mountain and past Higo School.

The Shippy Lane crossed the North Fork and the Platte River. That's where the lanes ended in those days. We followed the road to where it turns up the Platte Hill, there we turned southwest up Turkey Hollow and hit the cutoff road which we followed over Peterson Ridge where we hit Hiway 14 and so to the Home Ranch.

As we got toward the head of Turkey Hollow we hit a little green grass and those yearlings in the drag spread out. Bill and I were losing ground and riding as hard as we could. In the sage brush I ran across a dump. I got off and found an empty gallon can and was putting some rocks in it when Bill rode up and says, "Kid, tie that old wash boiler on my rope." I did and got back on old Sage. I went one way while Bill went the other and we took up the slack in a hurry.

That was a sight when we came over Peterson Ridge. There were cattle strung out just turning into the Home Ranch gate.

Quite a day for my first day, but it hadn't ended yet. I was still to meet Katy or "Maw" Freeman. She and her husband Charley contracted the Home Ranch for The Big Horn. I had heard of her from other cowboys, and gathered that she had her bluff in. I'd better explain here that I still had my first beard and I had got it trimmed up when I had a barber shop haircut. It was with some concern that I walked in to supper, where there were probably a dozen men eating at a long table. As I

Me at the Home ranch with my first beard.

walked in Maw Freeman said, "You with the beard go to the far end of the table." Charlie sat at the other end and she sat on the side toward the kitchen. I gladly went to the far end of the table.

The reason for taking the yearlings to the Home Ranch was that they had to be dipped for scabies, as all cattle had to be in North Park. In 1919 several outfits had bought scaby bulls at Stock Show which caused an outbreak of scabies. So they built dipping outfits at Lake Creek and the Home Ranch complete with vats, steam boilers to heat the dip, vat drain pens, and corrals big enough to hold many cattle. We were to dip all the yearlings, all the bulls (just under 200), and all the stock cows on the south end, a total of over 3,500 Big Horn cattle as I recall. There were 20 to 25 men, a full bunkhouse, most of the cow outfit, the ranch crew, plus a dipping crew. It was decided that a beef should be butchered and a big fat dry cow was selected. Now there was a place built to hang a beef, but it was not in the corral at the Home Ranch (and we hadn't even got

there yet). They corralled the cow, but instead of shooting it
and dragging it out to be lifted, it was roped and led out to the
butchering sight. There was a young dude there from back in
the cornbelt who wanted to shoot the cow. He shot and missed
the cow but shot the rope in two. Away went the cow. By the
time she was recaptured and returned to the butcher site, she
was hot and mad. That turned out to be some of the worst beef
I ever tried to eat. As a whole we ate very good at Katy's table.
She was a good cook and took a lot of pride in her cooking.

Dipping was all overseen by a U.S. Veterinarian, Dr.
Burnstine, who tested the lime and sulfur dip for strength and
temperature. He also saw that the cattle were soaked the proper
length of time. There were overhead gates that we could let
down to hold the cattle in the mixture. There were a number of
men along the vat with long handled hooks that we could hook
under the neck to stop a cow, or hook under a leg to turn over
if they got upside down. After they came out of the vat there
were two drain pens where we held the cattle until most of the
dip had run off and back into the vat. When one pen got full we
would use the other pen, and empty the first before the second
one got filled.

A coal fired boiler produced steam that was piped under
the dip to heat it. I think we dipped all the cattle twice. I do
recall that we had to dip the bulls either six times seven days
apart or seven times six days apart because the bulls were the
ones that scabies had been found on for sure. Also we dipped
cattle for neighbors who were going to run on the Forest with
The Big Horn. We dipped bulls for neighbors too. Dub Trownsell
had a dipping vat across the road from the Home Ranch, but it
was not fired up all the time, so we dipped bulls that were dipped
at both places. We dipped everything twice in two weeks, probably 3,500 to 4,000 head, then we held the bulls at the Home
Ranch until the required dippings were completed.

Katy Freeman did not have a hired girl but she did have an
Eastern boy helping her who washed dishes and helped out.

Also Katy had a friend from Walden, a blond twin who used to come to the ranch for supper. One time when she came before supper this Eastern kid rushed up to the bunkhouse and changed into a suit of clothes that he had. After supper when he came back to the bunkhouse Bill Angel asked, "Did you make an imprint?"

Along in May an annual event occurred, the Old Homestead opened. Some of the cowboys were going and said, "Kid if you will get that beard shaved off we will take you along." It was itching so I agreed and got a shave in Walden when we went. It so happened the blond twin went to the dance with Frank Hoskinson. When they got into the front seat she asked, "Is that guy with the beard still out there?" Frank answered, "He is in the back seat." That ended that conversation quick!

A good time was had by all and we got back in time for breakfast. I got a surprise when I walked in for breakfast. Katy Freeman said, "Say, you're a good looking kid without that beard! You can come to the head of the table." So I went and sat at Charley's left. From then on when I was there for a meal that was my place.

Maw Freeman later told me of the feud Hank McDaniels and George McGuire had when Freemans lived on the Shafer Ranch before coming to the Home Ranch. Hank and George were boarding there and riding out from there. One day Maw noticed they were not speaking so she took one of them aside and asked what was the matter. "The son of a bitch is stealing my cigarettes," was the reply. She took the other one off, asked the same question, and got the same answer. So she got them together and said, "We are going to the bunkhouse!" Hank's bed was on one side of the bunkhouse and George's was on the other side. Each had a stand by their bed, with an open carton of cigarettes on it, one of Lucky Strikes, the other Camels. She said, "One of you climb up into the attic." Sure enough there were the missing cigarettes, where a pack rat had taken them! It turned out alright and Hank and George went to Arizona one winter. Hank told me of hunting for lemon pie as they traveled. Finally when they found a place with lemon pie the waitress asked, "Do you want a piece?" They said, "No, we want the whole pie!"

The bunkhouse on the Shafer Ranch.

When we moved from Lake Creek to the Home Ranch, Fred Egry brought my bedroll and clothes. He told me, "Kid, you had better learn to roll that bed of yours, it looked like it had been gathered by a scatter rake." I took the hint.

As soon as the cattle and bulls had been dipped twice, the cattle were scattered out but the bulls had to be kept there for another month. I was chosen to herd the bulls in the daytime, and corral them nights in the dipping corrals. There were 195 bulls as near as I can recall. Herefords mostly, altho' Jack White, the manager of The Big Horn, had bought two carloads of Shorthorn bulls. They were ill natured and I got personally acquainted with many of them during my bull herding days.

Eventually we got the dipping of the bulls done and split them. The north end bulls were taken to the bull pastures at the Shafer Ranch and Bill Angel helped me take the south end bulls to Clover Valley.

Breakfast was always at 6 am on The Big Horn Ranches. Dinner was at noon and supper at 6 pm I would eat breakfast, catch a horse, and turn the bulls out of the corrals. That was the easy part. Herding them was not hard. After that I would go to the house for dinner. Then about 4 o'clock I would earn my pay getting those bulls all into the corral. They did not care for those corrals where they had been dipped many times and they would fight to stay out. The one that got whipped never ran towards the pens and I'd always lose ground. I tried penning part of them as there were plenty of pens, but whenever I started with part of the bulls away would go the rest to the far side of the field, a matter of a couple of miles. I did get a break tho'. The calves in Lake Creek were to be branded and Bill Angel volunteered to herd bulls if I wanted to go branding. I accepted.

When I got ready to move to Lake Creek to brand I put some clean clothes and a shaving outfit in my bed roll. Then I snapped them up and folded them ends to middle and threw the bundle on one of the saddle horses. Then I threw a square hitch on it and turned the horse out with the bunch. This was the usual procedure for moving.

There must have been near a thousand pairs in Lake Creek. We would cut off a bunch, corral and brand the calves, then trail them to the free range, a distance of a couple of miles. There we would pair them up, and repeat the procedure. It seems that we branded for four days.

I, being the kid, was a calf rassler, along with a guy called Spooks. I do know that we rassled a lot of calves. Those days blackleg was the only vaccine given at branding time and there was nothing done about the horns then.

After the horse Sage, I was given a sorrel horse named Blondy and a brown horse whose name I have forgotten. Hank McDaniels had the best string of horses because he broke them himself. He used to lend me a horse now and then, but always said, "Now don't get attached to him." I thought that Hank was tough on his horses, but 12 years later when I came back after World War II there was still old Tommy that Hank had broke.

If there was a cow in sight she had Tommy's attention. Hank broke horses for a lot of North Parkers.

The old MacFarlane place belonged to a man by the name of Keoughan. The Big Horn rented the Keoughan ranch. Keoughan had a few cattle, and 50 or 75 head of horses, most of which were at the Home Ranch. There was supposed to be a broke saddle horse among them that had gone sour. I being short of horses inquired about him. One day when we were not dipping and had a bunch of cows to move, it was suggested they bring the horses in and I'd ride him. Nobody seemed to know for sure which horse. They roped a bay horse that was

Branding at Lake Creek in 1934. Hank McDaniels branding, Me, Fred Egry, Bert Wilcox, and Spooks.

not halter broke and I said, "I don't think that is the right horse." Fred Egry, the boss, said, "Go ahead and ride him."

Hank helped me get a hackamore and my saddle on him, I mounted and Hank turned him loose. He was no green colt! That old pony turned the crank from the first jump and in due time I was bucked off in the gravel up by the dipping corrals. Hank gathered him up, I remounted, and Hank led him until we got into the meadow. There I asked to be turned loose. He bucked three more times. The last time my saddle was getting loose and I quit him as me and the saddle were going over his withers. The score was two for him and two for me. When we got in I took my saddle off, offered the hack reins, and asked "Who wants him?" Nobody. So I turned him loose. Later, when I was alone, I caught the right horse, saddled him up, and mounted with no help. He buried his head between his front feet and bawled real loud as he bucked and spun not very far off the ground. That was it, he never gave any more trouble.

The horse was probably 9 years old and tough as a boot. I ended up naming him Snort and he turned out to be a good

Me on Snort at the Home Ranch bunkhouse in 1934.

horse. Even tho' nobody could remember what the horse looked like, it seems now that a hell of a lot was known about this horse. Among other things they said Snort could not be roped off of. Later, I started roping sage brush and pulling it up.

Coming from the dry lands I had no experience with soap holes. Soap holes are holes in the Earth's crust where alkali mud oozes through. Some are small and some are many feet across. Like I said I had no experience with them, but I had heard plenty. Like about when one guy had shot another, and tried to stuff his body in a soap hole in Baker Draw (I read about the trial before ever coming to North Park). When we got done branding at Lake Creek I was to ride back to the Home Ranch and had to cross Baker Draw. I worried somewhat about soap holes but when I got there I decided that the horse knew a hell of a lot more about soap holes than I did. I sat very lightly on him as he took me across safely. By trial and error I learned about soap holes, and I still don't like them.

Some time after the Lake Creek branding Hank McDaniels got himself fired (something about marrying an ex-housekeeper of Mrs. White's). That left 7 or 8 of the best horses on the outfit

to be divy'd up. I did not get any of Hank's horses at that time,
I did get a couple of horses that Bert Wilcox had named Spider
and Maggot. Spider was a long barreled horse that rode mighty
rough. Maggot was a snorty black horse that had to be roped if
anyone was to catch him. Some of The Big Horn horses could
be caught, most had to be roped.

Bert Wilcox was a fine man somewhat older than the rest
of the crew, quiet around stock. I enjoyed riding with him and
he told me many things about the country as we rode, as well
as the old days. Bert had among his string this Maggot horse
that was fast and hard to rope. Bert was somewhat slow with a
rope (not much smoke on his rope). Many mornings we would
get saddled up ready to go, but Bert would still be roping at that
Maggot horse. We wouldn't dare help him and wouldn't dare
ride off without him like they had done me that first morning!

In the 1930's The Big Horn did not raise any saddle horses.
They bought horses, some good, some not so hot. I recalled a
Jack horse that had come from Jack Lundy, an Abe horse from
Abe Lenhart, and EY from E.Y. Gibbs. There were several
bunches of wild horses that they got, maybe from Rout County
or The Red Desert. But that was later.

The south end consisted of the Home Ranch, the Keoughan,
the School Section, Clover Valley, and lots of leased pasture.
The north end consisted of the Hanson Ranch, the Boettcher
Ranch, Lake Creek, the Shafer, and the Hill Ranch. I was always considered a south end cowboy. Until after WWII.

There were well over 100,000 acres of North Park that was
free range when The Taylor Act was passed in 1934. None of
the land was fenced and there were no cattle guards on any
roads either. There were horses year round, and cattle and sheep
from early spring to late fall. That made for plenty of room and
very little feed.

The Big Horn ran from Baker Draw to the Roaring Fork at
Manvilles clear up to the Butler School. Manvilles and Lathams
shared this piece of country too.

The first time I rode out to check this piece of free range over next to Beaver Creek I saw a guy fixing fence. I rode up with the brand side of my horse toward him. He was a big loud Dutchman and he proceeded to tell me how The Big Horn was trying to eat him out! Finally he ran down and asked, "Who do you work for?" And I admitted that I rode for The Big Horn. Then he backed up somewhat and admitted that his fences were not all that good.

The cowboys generally did not carry lunches, but Katy Freeman volunteered to fix me a lunch anytime. So I used to say, "I'll need a good lunch today, I'm going to ride over towards the Dutchman's." She would say, "You stay on your horse, you can cuss him but don't get off!" I never did have any more words with the Dutchman, in fact, I never saw him again that spring.

Then I settled down riding lanes. The Big Horn cattle on the south end had been dipped but the north end cattle would not be dipped until fall. 1934 was dry but there was green feed in the lanes where irrigating went on. The North End free range came down to the county road, about a mile and a half north west of the Platte Bridge. Cattle could go either toward the bridge, or west across the North Fork to the Hell Creek lane, around Butte Lakes and south. One day I would ride the Platte lanes, the next day the Hell Creek lanes. The cattle that had been dipped showed a gray tinge from the lime and sulfur dip, so I could tell them and work them south. The cattle I found that were not dipped I'd push back north on their free range.

As spring wore on I was to bring those dipped cattle and put them in the Staples pasture at the southwest corner of the range. That added 10 or 12 miles to my day. That was a long way from the Roaring Fork, the last water, to the Staples pasture with cattle. I'd get mighty dry some of those June days. I would get to Newcomb Creek and take on a fill laying down on my belly to drink. I'd done this a couple of days before, this time I hit the creek a couple hundred yards up stream, and saw

a dead horse right in the middle of the creek! Too late to worry
about it. Then I understood the story of two cowboys who were
moving cattle and getting dry when they came on a puddle.
The cattle waded in and were drinking when one cowboy lay
right down behind the cattle and proceeded to drink. The other
one went around to the far side to drink, then said "Why don't
you come over here where it ain't muddy to drink?" The other
one answered, "Hell, it don't make any difference where I start,
I'm going to drink it all anyway!"

I finally got cattle enough gathered and took them to Clover Valley, up the lane west past Turner's and Johnson's, and
into the northwest corner of Clover Valley.

Cars didn't travel so fast in those days, so we turned cattle
out on Hiway 14. They would drift up to Clover Valley and go
in just above the Colorado Creek bridge. We were not the only
ones to do this. John Peterson, Dub Trownsell, and Ordway
Mellen all turned cattle out to drift up country. There were cattle
on that stretch of the Hiway for several weeks each spring. They
mixed some but most of them were to go onto the Forest where
they could mix anyway.

We also moved cattle up the way I did those cattle from
Staples pasture but they couldn't drift up that way because there
was not a lane that went all the way along the Doran and across
the Johnson pastures which The Big Horn had leased at that
time for The Big Horn sheep outfit.

Along in July of 1934 after the dipping and calf branding
were done and the cattle were on the Forest, I had word from
my brother Dutch. He and I were in partnership on a dry-land
farming venture and Dutch needed help. So my first stint as a
Big Horn cowboy came to an end.

"*There was a fellow that lived way up in the hills that used to make moonshine. One evening there were several men around the table playing cards and sipping moonshine. There were several hounds asleep on the floor when one of the men cracked a loud fart. Those dogs popped up, looked at each other, and ran out the door! Someone finally asked 'What hit those dogs?' The moonshiner laughed and said 'I have been knocking the hell out of them for farting in the house!'*"

—a Bill Angel favorite

On Top

During the winter of 1934-1935, I came back and trapped at Johnsons after the harvest was finished on the dry land.

I started a diary on January 1st, 1935. Here are some notes from that diary.

Johnson's silver foxes got distemper and they lost many before they found out what it was. They contacted Dr. Withers in Denver. He got ahold of a Dr. Hermann a veterinarian also of Denver and the two of them came as far as they could by car, probably to Coalmont. They brought vaccine for the foxes. They were met by team and sled. Dr. Hermann vaccinated all the foxes and they quit dying. I sold Dr. Hermann a red fox fur for $18.

We continued working on the new house and on April 17th we moved Maw Johnson in. Then on April 29th we moved our beds from the bunkhouse into the upstairs of the new house.

Otto Johnson never moved into their new house, he had his bedroom in the old cabin, in the northeast corner, and was happy there. He passed away there on August 11th, 1935. I was with him at the end and I felt that I had lost a true friend that morning.

Another entry. It snowed 19 days in April. It snowed or rained 28 days in May! We fed with a sled until May 14th, that's over 7 months feeding by sled!

The new Johnson house.

I went to Albert Manville's on May 20th and he hired me to ride for The Big Park Association for $65 a month. I was to start about the 1st of July and ride into fall until October 1st when we were to start gathering the cattle.

I went back out home on June 7th. On June 12th, I had my first plane ride. Harold "Had" Gunn was in the Army Air Force had stopped to see his folks and landed on the baseball diamond, west of Bensons. He was flying a two seater fighter plane with the machine gun synchronized to fire through the propeller.

There were controls in each cockpit. I got into the rear one and fastened the seat belt. I reached down and felt a rod that I could not pull loose and said, "I've got a handful of mane, let's go!" We did, and he climbed, then did dives and barrel rolls. I never looked anywhere but at my feet until we leveled out. When I did look, we were upside down. But in spite of all that we landed safely.

One Sunday we went to Earl Andersons, the diary says. Paul Crain, Paul Carney, Dutch and I rode saddle broncs. Another Sunday we were back to Andersons. That was the day Paul Carney tried bull dogging and got into considerable cactus that had to be pulled out. He had to take his pants down for that operation!

On June 28th I came back to North Park. I went to Steamboat on the 4th of July and started riding for The Big Park Association on the 5th of July.

Here I would like to give you a little background of the Big Park Association. The North Park Stock Growers Association was formed in March of 1899 at Hebron Colorado. Some 10,000 acres of school land in Grand County were leased from the State Land Board and two steer pastures were fenced, one known as the Swede Lease the other as the 2-bar. The steers were taken over early and put in the pastures then the cows were taken over in the latter part of June. According to Ordway Mellen, the Big Horn cowboys would start at Red Hill in the north end. Everyone along the way would join in and push all the cattle west of the Illinois River across into Middle Park and onto the State Lease and other open range. They would go home for the 4th. of July then return to Middle Park, have the calf roundup and brand the calves. Then they'd all go back and home and hay.

The North Park Stock Growers hired a range rider right away in 1899. The first was J.C. Trimbell, followed by Ralph Coyte in 1900, then Joe Graham who was range rider for several years until around 1908 or 9 when John Peterson rode. John rode until 1915 when the state land in Middle Park was allotted to the Middle Park ranchers and the North Park cattle were run on the forest there.

Although the two steer pastures were still held in 1919 there is no record of a range rider from 1915 to 1919. The cattle were pushed up all along the forest from the north edge of Middle Park to Wyoming on the north, over the top, and down Walton Creek as far as Storm Mountain and Fish Creek Canyon. Then down Mad Creek and into Horsethief Park. It is reported there were 2,000 cattle gathered off that country in 1919, the first year John Burns was range rider. Cattle were gathered on the Chedsey Flats south of the Butler School house (those were sagebrush flats then) where they were sorted and sent home to many owners. John Burns came back from World War I in 1919 and was hired by Bill Latham as Range Rider. He and many that followed him used the Buffalo Pass Ranger Station for a camp until about 1930.

Bill Latham hired John Burns in 1919 and Bill Latham eventually headed the Big Park Association. Probably that was when the association was formed but there is very little that can be found out about it. I do know there was a range rider hired for Buffalo Pass from 1919 to 1942. A complete list is not available but here is what I was able to find. Besides John Burns, these were known to have rode up there, some for more than one year: Al Manville, Irving Graves, Bert Wilcox, J.W. Mackey, and Bill Latham's nephew known as Stuttering Bill Latham. He was there for 3 or 4 years prior to when I went to work in 1935. I rode through 1941 and was the last, if not the best.

This quote came from a supervisor's report on the Routt Forest in 1910: "The high range has been proven useless as cattle range on account of the short season, early snows and flies." Right on top of that it says the supervisor recommended a drift fence from Buffalo Pass to Rabbit Ears be built to hold back The Big Horn cattle from drifting into the Yampa and Elk Rivers! This fence was built in 1911 not to Rabbit Ears but to Buffalo Park: some 14 miles of 4 wire, creosote post, government specification fence. The Steamboat Pilot of 1911 reported that the fence was to be the deadline between the cattle and the sheep!

I was never told that when I rode that range from 1935 thru 1941. In 1935 when I started riding there were some brace panels that still stood east of the Buffalo Pass Ranger station and west of Summit Lake about a mile. That fence did cost a bundle of money tho'. I saw a statement from the Forest Service to

UNITED STATES DEPARTMENT OF AGRICULTURE
FOREST SERVICE
ROUTT NATIONAL FOREST

P
Projects.-L-49.

STEAMBOAT SPRINGS, COLO.

September 1, 1911.

Mrs. Grace Peterson,

Hebron, Colorado.

Dear Madam:

Further reference is made to your letter of August 16.

I am in receipt of a letter from the District Forester which states that the Rabbit Ear Drift Fence was constructed by contract, the actual cost being $2,240. The cost of wire purchased from the American Steel & Wire Company was $668.25, making a total cost of $2,908.25, or $200.58 per mile, the length of the fence being a little over 14½ miles. A slight additional sum should be added to this for the cost of freight on wire and cost of staples, the latter being included in a number of smaller bills at Steamboat Springs which are included in the cost of experiments. , The cost of the experiments on this fence, including treatment of posts and some construction to withstand snow, was $916.43. These experiments cost $63.00 per mile. The total cost of the fence including the experiments, was $3,824.68 or $263.77 per mile.

I trust this is the information you desire.

Very truly yours,

Forest Supervisor.

Statement from the Forest Service to Grace Peterson.

Grace's grandmother, Grace Peterson. We were not able to find out how much of the cost of this fence was paid by Grace Peterson, but it is said to have been considerable.

It was poor planning from the start. At Buffalo Pass, the fence should have been half a mile east, that would have put a larkspur patch that was poisonous to cattle but not sheep into the sheep range instead of the cattle range. The fence was not a success. The snow mashed it down so they tried letting it down in the fall but finally gave up.

By 1918 the powers that be decided to try "common use" on the range: the sheep were to use the canyons and the cattle were to use the high, wet, open meadows. As far as we can determine this was the first time common use was tried on the National Forest. By 1919 the supervisor reported it was working "nicely." That was the first year the Big Park Association had a rider up there. John Burns stayed in the Buffalo Pass Ranger station then, and tho' it was on the sheep side of that folly fence it was used as a cow camp until about 1930 when the camp was moved east on top of the ridge south of Summit Lake, and into a tent set up on a wooden frame some 30 inches high. This frame was left in place all winter but the ridge pole was a 2x4" that was removable, and was set on end next to a big spruce tree for the winter. The stove was stashed under that same tree. This camp later became my camp when I rode there.

The Big Park Grazing Association. Newcomb Park and Big Park were one and the same. When I started riding for them in 1935 there were four permittees. The Big Horn brand =M, Albert Manville brand N̂A , Bill Latham brand Z̲H̲, and the Carl Erickson brand 7̲V̲. Each held a permit for 250 cattle. The Big Horn always put out cows and calves. Some of the others put out some yearlings, to make up their count. Today it would have been called a pool, then that name was not in use.

July first was turnout date. The Big Horn usually turned out at The Little Grizzly Creek Ranger Station, Lathams up Chedsey Creek and Al Manvllle turned out Colbern Draw, and Newcomb Creek, Carl Erickson kept his cattle in most of July, to get as many cows bred to his own bulls possible, then we would go directly on top via The Buffalo Pass Road. The other

I arrive at the tent camp.

cattle were drifted up Chedsy Creek and Newcomb Creek. The bulls were turned out shortly after the 4th of July.

I was supplied with about six horses. They were allowed, I think, $15 each for furnishing horses. A camp was also furnished, complete with a tent, a stove, and a set of box springs.

The camp was to be moved up as soon as the snow on the Continental Divide (or "on top") had melted enough that Al Manville could get up there with a 4-horse team, carrying a couple tons of salt and the camp. Until then I rode out from Johnsons and Manvilles.

On July 23rd Al Manville moved the camp to the top. Forest Ranger Sam Orr and I rode over the range and were on top when Al got there so we all set up my new home for the summer. The wooden tent frame was still there, so we stretched the tent on top of that and made the tent high enough that you could stand up in it. There was an old laundry stove that was left up there under a big spruce tree along with a 3/4 box spring for the bed. There was no corral or horse pasture but they did furnish me oats to help me catch my horses. I always had a bell or two to hang on the horses so I'd know which way to go to find them come morning. I might say here I got so I would hear those bells in my sleep. It seemed I could sleep all night but would know which way the horses had gone that night.

To start with, I hobbled all the horses. Then as I learned how each horse adjusted to camp life, many did not have to be hobbled.

More about the camp and why it was where it was. It was south of Summit Lake on Buffalo Pass. Buffalo Pass is 10,250 feet elevation. My camp was uphill south of that, right over the ridge so I could look across the canyon and into the larkspur patch I was guarding. There was timber on that hillside and I could see where any cattle were before I went across to get them out.

Larkspur is poisonous to cattle and is bad in wet weather. Even a heavy dew would react with the plant making it poisonous to cows. In the 7 years that I rode there I only lost two cows in that patch. One died near the bottom of the canyon and a bear or bears moved in and cleaned her up in about three nights although I never did see a bear. The other cow I lost was a Big Horn cow that got hooked on larkspur. She and her calf would show up nearly every day. I took her south to Longs lake and the next morning she was back. I took her over and down the head of Mad Creek and back again. Then I took her down off the top, and put her next to the cattle in the Crosby pasture. She came back one wet night and finally got too much larkspur and died over north of Dinosaur Lake. A sheepherder came around a big rock and this cow charged him. She ran a short way and died. I never saw her calf again. I suppose that he came home as a bum.

After staying at camp overnight Ranger Orr and I rode along the top and went over Mt. Ethel across a lot of snow, down past Rainbow Lake to Slide Lake, and into Colburn Draw.

There we ran across some cattle trespassing. They belonged

to a Dane by the name of Chris who had a ranch on Beaver Creek. He had asked me when I started riding if I would turn him in if he turned a few cattle out on The National Forest. I was young and green and wanted to stay in with the neighbors so I had told him, "I'll not turn you in, but some of the guys I'm riding for might." I knew that Ranger Orr was going to ride that allotment and I told him so.

Chris said, "Can't you miss Colburn Draw?"

I told him, "Orr is riding the range. I am riding with him. Where he goes is up to him."

When Ranger Orr saw those cattle, we hunted up Mr. Chris and had him move his cattle home. He never tried to trespass again. I don't think he had over 20 or 25 cattle out there. But Chris never liked me from then on.

We had pushed cattle up Round Mt. way and up Chedsey Creek considerably before we got the camp up, so I worked at pushing over the top. We never tried to run any cattle around Buffalo Pass road on top. When we would bring cattle up Chedsey Creek, we would come out on top right at Summit Lake, but we never dropped cattle there. We always took them south of the larkspur canyon. All the cattle from Spring Creek and Colburn Draw had to be pushed south across Beaver Creek and into Newcomb Park then up Round Mountain trail and out at the head of Mad Creek on the Western Slope. By the end of summer they would be moved south of camp onto Fish Creek.

One time when I was first up there I was cleaning up the upper end of Chedsey Creek. It was cloudy and drizzly, those cattle spooked and we were around in the breaks. I got lost and finally came out at Summit Lake, and nothing looked right. I rode to camp and it was turned around until I went inside the tent and shut my eyes. When I opened them again, things were square.

In the fall of 1935 Al Manville's help went back to Kansas after we were pretty well done gathering. Al was alone and was milking around 16 cows so I helped him. I was still riding look-

Me and Albert Manville at his place.

ing, but I helped with the chores. It got to snowing but we couldn't get away to ride the top to look for tracks and pack the camp down. When Al's help returned Al and I took 2 pack horses and headed for the top. There was considerable snow by the time we got on top by way of Round Mountain trail and Al's cattle had ranged west of the top there so he wanted to make a circle to look for tracks. I took the pack horses and went to camp, afraid of what I would find as the snow was deep. I arrived about an hour before sundown and saw a pitiful sight. The snow had gotten heavy enough to split the ridgepole and the tent frame was full of snow. At first the only thing that I found was a small skillet so I started bailing snow out with it. Next I got in far enough to get the wash basin then when I found the water bucket I was able to bail the snow out so I could wire the ridge pole together and set the tent up. I had been cold when I got there but by the time I got the tent up I was hot, under the collar too! When Al rode in I unloaded.

(Forgetting he was my boss) I told him if he was going to stay all night he had better promise to build a cabin for future use. He stayed.

My cabin on top in the Fall of 1941. Bare ground.

My cabin in the Spring of 1942, taken by some of the Turner kids after I'd gone into the service.

In the summer of 1939 one of the Osborns came up with a load of lumber, tin for the roof, a door, and windows. They cut logs and laid them up and we had a cabin on top which I used and enjoyed the summer of 1940. The sad part was in the spring of 1941 The Big Horn sold the South End and the Forest permit went with the sheep outfit so there was no more Big Horn cattle grazing on that part of the Forest. Later I rode for Al Manville and Carl Erickson who ranged cattle in the low country. Some cattle drifted on top tho' so I used the cabin now and then when I was checking those cattle.

I have told how different outfits furnished horses for the range rider. I will introduce you to my first string. From The Big Horn I got Old Sage and a little sorrel horse by the name of Kid. Kid was born a wild horse and never quite got over it. He would kick. He never got me but it was embarrassing to have your horse kick somebody else. From Carl Erickson I got two horses: Moon, a good older black horse who got lame that first summer, and a dizzy bay mare we called Skeeter. From Al Manville I got a Jim Peterson horse by the name of Pete that Stutterin' Bill Latham had broke the year before. The only problem with Pete is that he would whirl away from you when you went to get on. He would try to buck too, but I always said he couldn't buck a wet saddle blanket off. Of course that fall Pete bucked me off. It was late and I was on top looking for cattle down west of my camp, I'd just come off the hill and was turned around in my saddle looking back. I had looked ahead earlier and seen a small stream. When Pete got to it he stopped. I never looked around, just grabbed him in the flank with my spur. He jumped that stream, hit a'bucking, and lost me before I could get straightened up. I got up and looked all around to see if anyone had seen me get bucked off. I was disappointed. I thought it would have been funny to see. I also got from Al a packhorse, Nig, to use until I got the salt on top scattered, and a brown horse name of Tony, not a great cow horse, but always pleasant to have around. At different times that first year these horses that quit the top went down to the fences hobbled, but only once. Those legs got pretty sore before they traveled those 7 or 8 miles. That Big Horn horse Kid didn't leave and really he was one horse that had to be roped. At first I hobbled him and would try to slip up close enough to rope him, then one morning that didn't work. I caught another horse and tried to rope him but I could not catch up with him hobbled! I ran him clear to the Ranger Station corral before I caught him. After that I put a chain about 3-feet long on one front foot then when he started running that would whip around his front legs and he would stop and throw his head up. I could toss a rope on him but he would not let me walk up to him unless he had a rope on him. Later that summer, after I had taken Al's Nig horse back, I believe they worked him in the hayfield.

I decided to go down near the Stratton sheep corrals (just south of where the Fish Creek Reservoir is now). There was some barb wire there that the sheepherders had rolled up, and put on some big rocks. This wire was left over from the fence that had been built in 1911 from Buffalo Pass to Buffalo Park, some 17 miles. I looked my horses over and decided that old Sage looked like a pack horse so I put a pack saddle with panniers on him and went down. I tied two rolls of wire together and threw them on. Sage bucked them off at least six or seven times before I could get them lashed down. After that I could pack him without too much trouble.

There was no shortage of room to look for horses. It was 6 miles east to the Ranger Station, about 10 miles west to a fence, and north or south there were no fences! Miles were hard to determine. There was an estimated township, Range 83W, that had not been surveyed then. Quite a change for an old kid that had been raised where everything was laid out in square sections.

I learned to live alone. "Well," I always said, "if you ain't good company to yourself, you probably ain't good company." Most of the time in the summer tho' there were some people around, sheepherders, camp movers, fishermen, and campers. Towards fall after the sheep people left and there weren't too many tourists I went 9 days without seeing another person. It was such beautiful country and I was occupied doing something I'd rather be doing than anything else in the world so I didn't miss people much. Time never got to be a problem. Oh sure, when it got to raining and the cattle moved and never bawled, then I had to ride to keep them out of the poison weed. I would get wet, but that wasn't all bad. Summer sure was a pleasure. I met many people from the trail crew that worked for the Forest Service and many Steamboat people that became lifelong friends, along with the sheep people that were up there.

In summers Maw Johnson kept a few guests. Somewhere about 1936 the Thor Groswolds stayed at Johnsons. How well I recall the first time I saw them! I was moving cattle, and they came along in a car. Thor had brought his boys who were like 6 or 8 years old. Those boys looked me over and wanted to know, "Are you a cowboy?" I allowed I was and they wanted to know where my gun was so I showed them my pistol from my chap pocket.

Thor had a ski factory in Denver along with an inventor partner who designed ski poles, binders, and so forth. Later that summer I was coming back from south one day late and ran across a couple of guys with camp stuff tied all around their saddles, and they told me of their woes. They had rented the horses from Johnny Williams in Steamboat and came up to Longs Lake the day before. They had hobbled the horses that night and found themselves afoot the next morning so they walked back and got the horses. I do not recall whether they had rode them up bareback or led them. They had just got packed up and were worrying about being left afoot again that night. So I said, "Come stay with me, my horses will not leave, and if yours do we will not be afoot." The older man turned out to be Marcellus Merrill, Thor Groswold's partner, who had grown up in Steamboat Springs and was showing his young friend The Rocky Mountains.

Marcellus was known as Celly, an inventor who had many inventions patented. Besides all the ski equipment, he had the patent on auto wheel balancing equipment and car frame straightening equipment. In fact, he had shops in Denver, Pueblo, and Des Moines, Iowa.

Celly loved to come to my camp. Not so much to fish or ride, but just to get away from it all. He would stay a week at a time and would rent a horse from Al Manville to come. He was handy around camp and would fix things. I did the cooking, which wasn't *all* bad after the first summer. Celly was a history buff and a good storyteller and my interest in things historical date pretty much from the time I met him. He always kept a flashlight and notebook handy. He'd wake up in the night, light the flashlight, write things in the notebook, put out the light, and go back to sleep. When I first started writing a column, I found myself doing the same thing many years later.

Along in the late 30's Celly's business was doing well and he said, "Let's buy a ranch and you run it." I said, "I know the ranch, The Big Horn has had it leased and it is for sale, good ranch, good water, and good pasture and it can be had for $38,000." He said "Just one thing, we won't raise cattle, we will raise buffalo and sell the meat to hotels who feed tourists, like the Stanley Hotel in Estes Park. Why, those dudes would pay as much as $2 a meal to be able to go home and tell that they had eaten buffalo."

I said, "Whoa! Buffaloes are hard to keep under fence, hard to handle, and we would get a skimpy calf crop."

I kept that attitude until I came back from WWII several years later when Celly said, "We sure missed the boat! There were no ration points on buffalo meat during the war."

There really is not a whole lot to tell about the cattle/sheep wars in North Park. When the first sheep came into North Park there was a sheep wagon parked on a ridge. A couple of young men riding for a cow outfit rode by in the daytime and noticed the wagon tongue was propped up off the ground. That night they rode up and tossed their ropes over the tongue and rode off down hill. One told me "That sheepherder had no sense of humor, he began shooting at us through the door with a 30-30!" It didn't take long for both to ride to one side and roll that sheep wagon down the hill.

As stated elsewhere most of the sheep that came into North Park were brought by cowmen that had gone broke in the 20's and 30's. They couldn't get financed for more cows but could get financed to buy sheep. They were cheaper and brought in two paydays a year: wool, then lambs.

The big sheep wars were on the Western Slope. I was told of them by a Big Horn cowboy who took part in some of them. He told of when the Little Snake River on the Colorado-Wyoming line was the deadline between the cattle men and the sheepmen and how the sheep would bed on the Wyoming side, get up and cross the river, graze until they were full, bed down then towards evening, graze again, then cross back into Wyoming full to again bed down for the night.

One time this cowman heard that green coffee beans were deadly poison for sheep. They proceeded to get a hundred pound sack, packed it on a pack horse, and spent the night placing the coffee beans around on rocks where the sheep would be sure to find them. The next day they watched with binoculars. Sheep came across, fed, bedded down, then got up and fed again, but nary a dead sheep could they see. Then they heard that saltpeter would kill sheep. They went through the same procedure with a hundred pounds of saltpeter. Again nary a dead sheep. Stories were as close as I ever came to a Cattle and Sheep War and I found sheep people were actually handy to have around.

There were several sheep outfits that ran near my camp. The Stratton Brothers, Abe and Tony, owners of The Leo Sheep Company out of Rawlins, Wyoming, ran 4 bands on the west slope from just north of the Buffalo Pass road south to about Longs Lake. Strattons also ran 4 bands north of Windy Gap around west of Red Canyon, and 2 bands over on Parkview above Rand. Vivions trailed through our allotment south to the vicinity of Rabbit Ears. The Cow Creek Sheep Company had an allotment for 2 bands that took in all of the headwaters of the South Fork of Mad Creek. These sheep outfits were all out of Rawlins. I got to know all of the Stratton help that were around our allotment. They were all Mexicans. They called themselves Mexicans and were proud of it. Every sheep outfit in those days that hired Mexicans had a head Mexican, Stratton's was Pablo Romero, The Big Horn's was Que, Mallon's was Carlos, and so on.

Strattons were all from Taos, New Mexico. Pablo had been coming up to that range since 1909 for Strattons. Pablo talked good English, and was quite well educated. Several of the older herders spoke very little English and I spoke very little Span-

Sorted lambs at the Stratton's corral in the early 1940's.

ish. All I had was one year of Spanish in high school, mostly self taught. They would talk in English as far as they could, then shift to Spanish. I would go as far as I could in Spanish, then shift to English. By the time we had visited 7 summers, we had developed quite a lingo but we understood each other.

I learned to cook on a campfire from those guys as they did all their cooking and baking on campfires. I ate many a good meal with them and they were always glad to have me stop for a meal.

They gave me a leg of lamb after they got to know who I was. I had a couple of Al Manvilles dogs with me most summers and I fed that first leg of lamb to the dogs. But after I had eaten lamb that those guys had fixed, I ate any lamb that they gave me. After that the dogs had to do on scraps and cornmeal mush. There was no such thing in those days as dog food!

One time I was over on the Stillwater and stopped at the sheep camp of a herder by the name of Emelio Roybal, a real happy-go-lucky Mexican who asked me to lunch to help him celebrate his good fortune. It seems a pack outfit had stopped

Porfidio Trujillo, Benito Sandavol, and me at their sheep camp near Fish Creek in 1939.

by on their way back to Steamboat and had given him a lot of food. As I recall there were roasting ears, cantaloupe, and all kinds of goodies. He really cooked up a meal! Towards the last he grabbed his head and said, "We got no chili."

I said, "We don't need chili with all we have to eat."

He replied, "On the Stratton Sheep Company you always have chili!" He proceeded to open a can and heat it up. Of course we never touched it, and he ended up feeding it to his dogs. I suspect that chili was sort of a staple dog food.

Those Mexicans baked tortillas in dutch ovens. There was one older man Benito Sandavol, one of my lingo friends, that made the best tortillas. The Mexicans would mix them in the top of the flour sack, work each into a ball, and then flip it between their hands until they had a disk the right size for the dutch oven. The fire for baking was good coals. They'd put the lid on the coals to preheat them along with the dutch oven, dig a hole about 6 inches deep the size of the oven, and shovel that hole part full of live coals. They'd use a pot-hook (a metal rod with a hook on one end with the other end bent back to form a handle) to set the dutch oven on the coals. Then they would put the tortillas in and put the lid on. The lid had a loop on top with a rim around the outer edge so hot coals could be heaped on top. The most trouble that I had baking with a dutch oven was too much heat on the bottom. My biscuits burned on the bottom and were pale on top.

I learned to cook at that camp. As I was growing up my brother Dutch did the cooking and I did dishes so I had to learn how to cook from scratch. For breakfast, I had coffee, fried eggs, fried bacon and hotcakes made from bisquick, which I used for both biscuits and hotcakes. I had never used condensed milk before and the only cereal that it could go on was spotted pup (rice cooked with raisins). I tried to keep baker's (store bought) bread on hand and when I ran out I had to build a campfire and bake in a dutch oven.

My larder consisted of a slab of bacon with rind, a half case of eggs, a half sack of potatoes, butter, peanut butter, jam in a half-gallon bucket, half a gallon of Crisco, pork and beans, other canned veggies, and canned fruit, flour, baking powder, and syrup. I always bought my grub from Sid Harris at Hebron. I'd keep my list from year to year, but I never saved one. I kept the eggs under the bed on the ground and I kept the bacon, butter, and any fresh meat in a meat sack, a Beemis seamless sack, that I hung on the north side of a big spruce tree. Any fish that I kept were put in a gallon bucket in the spring. I kept the bucket in the water by putting a rock on the lid to hold it down

Those Mexicans were real good to be around, they were all from Taos as was Pablo Romero. They told of one time in years past when a group of them were gathered and had gotten a mess of grouse, way out of season. In those days Forest Rangers were game wardens. A Forest Ranger happened by and was invited to eat. He did, then arrested the whole bunch. As I recall the fine was $10. One of those Mexicans told me about it saying, "All I got was a neck, and I had to pay my $10 too!"

I visited with them and got to know these people and something about how they lived in New Mexico. One time I asked, "How come if you all have that much in New Mexico, why are you up here herding sheep?"

They answered, "In New Mexico we have everything to live on but no money. We come to Wyoming to make money." It seems to me that their pay was around $60 a month, probably the camp movers got $5 a month more. Their board was furnished.

There were around a thousand head of ewes in a band, always with some black sheep. Some were numbered with paint, like from 10 to 50. Pablo Romero spent most of his time counting sheep. He would go from one band to another and count to find out if any were missing. The herders tried to get a count now and then of the blacks and numbered sheep. If they found there were sheep missing, they told the camp mover and he or someone else would help look for them. Coyotes got some sheep and occasionally a bear would get to bothering but there was never a trapper that worked on that range that I ever knew of.

It was a pleasure to watch Pablo count sheep. The sheep would come by 6 or 8 sheep wide. Pablo had a string of beads, 4 black, 1 white, and he would flip a bead every hundred. When he got done he could tell how many there were. There was another trick I saw them do. There were no calendars, so they would take a dry stick, whittle one side flat, and write 30 or 31 numbers on it. Every day they'd take the knife and whittle one number off.

There was a sheep driveway along the top. They would come in from Wyoming and go way down towards Steamboat, and work back up as the snow melted. It seemed they would get back up around the first part of August. I was always glad to see them because the sheep would work that canyon and eat all the leaves off the larkspur. The larkspur didn't bother the sheep at all and since the cattle would not get poisoned I didn't have to stay so close to camp.

*Supper at a sheep camp. From left to right: Porfidio Trujillo,
Benito Sandavol, and my friend, Marcellus Merrill.*

The lambs were taken off the ewes around the 5th of September. There was a corral down by where the Fish Creek Reservoir is now. They would take the wether lambs off where there was an alley with a cutting gate at the end. They cut by earmarks. When roughly a thousand lambs were cut off, they would combine the remaining sheep into 3 bands. Then they would meet the lambs from the head of Red Canyon and trail the wether lambs to Steamboat to ship to market. There was a saying, "If a herder's dogs were fat, his sheep will be fat." I use to go help when the lambs were cut off. I don't know how much help I was, but I got a lot of visiting done. A couple of Stratton sons generally would be there to help as it took lots of help to herd those lambs that had just been weaned.

Strattons ran a good outfit, they kept ewes until they were 7 years old. They had 6 earmarks, so the ewe lambs had the same earmark as the ewes that were to be culled that fall. The

sheep were branded with paint and they would touch up any
brands that needed it when they weaned. When they got the
lambs shipped, they would try to head back north by the middle
of September. It used to be whenever it would cloud up towards fall those Mexicans would say, "Pretty soon, I think so,
it is going to snow!" They never got enough snow to bother
while I was riding on top, but in years past there had been enough
snow to make it hard to travel. I do not recall a Mexican leaving during the summer, but when they got to where they changed
from teepees and pack horses to sheep wagons then there was
quite a turnover. Some would leave and some would come.
There was no water many places on the desert so they had to
have snow for the sheep to eat for water.

There were different ones there during the summers, I do
not recall all the names, but a couple I do recall were the Trujillo
brothers, Porfidio and Jesus. One time when Celly Merrill was
at my camp, the sheep moved up west of my camp and I had
not seen them move because I was riding. When I came in that
evening Celly told me that a Mexican had come by and wanted
us to come down for supper. I asked what his name was and
Celly couldn't remember so I asked what he looked like. He
said, "He was a young good looking Mexican."

So I said, "I'll bet that was Porfidio Trujillo."

Celly asked, "Is that a man's name?" Well, it was.

Those Mexicans were good cooks, when they fried potatoes in a dutch oven they would add a can of chilies when the
potatoes were nearly done. That was an improvement over the
spuds that I cooked–and fried spuds were a staple in my diet.
I never tried to cook beans up there. At over 10,500 feet elevation water wasn't all that hot when it started to boil. I did cook
rice, the first time I put a kettle on, it swelled until I had rice in
all three of my kettles.

I had better tell about my first gravy. Just before I ordered
groceries Al Manville told me, "Get some dried beef, then when
you need a quick meal, make gravy." Jack Ball who was at
Johnsons that summer came up to my camp to stay all night,

that evening I decided to make gravy. This dried beef came in a glass, in thin strips. I got the beef in a kettle and got it to boil. When I went to add the flour, I was stumped. I asked Jack, "How much flour should I put in?"

He said, "About a cupful ought to be about right." This I did, but I couldn't stir it quick enough and I had to feed it to the dogs. Jack went back and told Maw Johnson about it and she told the neighbor women. I had several of them ask if I had made any more gravy. I had an advantage. I could feed my mistakes to the dogs or bury them, which I did a lot of as I learned to cook. I fed the dogs scraps and every now and then I'd cook a batch of cornmeal mush. I learned to live off the land. Besides those legs of lamb that I fell heir to, I caught many trout, and I carried a .22 pistol in one chap pocket to shoot porcupines and grouse with.

I never ate the porcupines, but I did eat the grouse. As soon as the young got big enough, they made good eating, as did the trout. There were some holes on the Stillwater, (now named Granite Creek) up towards Grizzly Lake that were in a peat bog and always looked like manure water. You could not see into it, but I discovered native trout lived in them. I was never much of a fly fisherman but I could manage spinners, brass spinners on bright days and silver spinners on cloudy days, and was always able to catch some fish for camp.

One time several of us were riding down Chedsey Creek. I think we had been pushing cattle up when a bunch of grouse flew up and some lit in trees. Charlie Latham said, "I wish I had a gun." I had a pistol of sorts in my chaps pocket which I produced. Charlie shot it empty and that grouse never blinked an eye. I reloaded and Frank Hoskinson shot that one dry and hit a couple of branches near the grouse but it still sat. The third time I shot. I pulled down and hit the limb that the grouse was sitting on and it flew away.

Frank said, "You are a lot of help! Just when we get things cleared away so we can do something you scare the bird away!" There were many grouse in the 30's, especially in the fall when the wild currants were on. There was a small draw north of the Buffalo Pass Ranger Station where the currants were plentiful where I have seen literally hundreds of grouse at one time. How times change! In the late 40's I led a pack party up Red Canyon across the top to Buffalo Pass and down to Strawberry Park and we only saw two grouse the whole trip!

I never hunted Ptarmigan, but there were several broods raised among the Shining Rocks above Big Park. I liked to watch them, but come to think of it, I never saw a Ptarmigan in the winter when they were white. Even in all the skiing I did.

Porcupines were quite numerous. Stock, both cattle and horses, were forever smelling of a porky and coming up with a nose full of quills. Dogs too. Porkys lived in pine trees in the winter and ate bark damaging the trees, so I shot them on occasion. Whenever old Pup, the dog that followed me, found a porky on the ground he'd bark. But if the porky started to climb a tree, old Pup would nail him and get a face full of quills. I'd shoot the porky then get the pliers that I carried in the other chap pocket and pull the quills out of old Pup's nose.

One time I was down in Carl Erickson's Crosby pasture and met Frank Hoskinson. He had his saddle horn tied on the back of his saddle in a gunny sack. I asked," What happened to your saddle horn?" He said "I'm a good rider, I don't need a saddle horn."

It turned out he had run across one of Erickson's horses that was not halter broke but had a nose full of quills. Frank had roped it and that was what had happened to his saddle horn. He had it repaired, with a long bolt through the swell of his saddle. I suppose the horn was fastened in by the bolt. Anyway, as long as I knew him, it stayed that way and he never hesitated to rope anything.

When I went up on top I hobbled all my horses. As they got camp broke, I'd turn most of them loose. I always had oats for bait. I had some old bread pans that were good for a horse to eat from. In the morning I would take a pan of oats and a bridle or a hackamore and go to where the horses were. I'd give each a bite of oats, unhobble the others, ride one bareback, and take them all to camp where I'd leave them while I would ride out on my daily rounds.

I never got the same horses back any year that I rode the top. But I always got one or two back that were camp broke which helped.

One year I got the bright idea that I wanted all big horses and I got my wish. That was how this dry-lander found out that the higher up you get, the thicker the branches are.

Hippo was a Big Horn horse that was snorty but harmless. He was not much of a cow horse, but he would get you there and back and he could be packed and shot off of. Whenever I got a sour bull that would get in the willows, or down timber, and challenge you to come get him, I would borrow old man Johnson's sawed off shotgun and we would have a movement. I took a notion to teach Hippo to picket. I had a rope 40 or 50 feet long that I put on a front foot with half of a hobble, and tied the other end to a good sized log. I left in the afternoon and went south of camp. Hippo was where I had left him. But when I got back to camp, no Hippo. It was late and I followed where he had drug the log, which was some rotten, and had hit a rock and broke it up to where the rope had come off. It rained hard that night and I stayed in camp. The next morning not a track was left. I went down towards the Ranger Station, but there were no tracks either south, north, or in between, so I went back to camp and started again the next morning. I followed the road until where it turned north and rode straight into the timber for a mile or more until I heard a horse whinny. There was Hippo with the picket rope tangled in some brush and wrapped around a tree so's the rope never could pull out of the brush. He had eaten all the huckleberries off as far as he could reach them. I was glad to find him, but he was gladder to see me. It took a couple of days to get him filled up, and he never left camp or the other horses again.

Picketing Hippo and trying to build a horse pasture were some of the things I tried those first and second summers.

One summer I had a Big Horn horse named Jake that left me afoot. Jake was a sorrel horse that had a hip down but that didn't bother him. He was a good, faithful horse. We had moved the camp up and it was set up, but I had not stayed in it yet. I was pushing cattle up Chedsey Creek on Jake when I got above the falls near sundown. I decided I'd go to camp and stay the night because it was a lot closer than riding back to Manville's ranch. I had never had Jake at camp before so I let him eat until dark. I had no halter up there yet so I tied Jake up with my lariat rope. My rope was stiff and came untied. Jake left me afoot with a brand new pair of boots that were tight. I was sure Jake had gone down the way we had came up, so I headed down the road. Those boots got so hot that every stream I'd come to I would wade in. I could almost feel the steam rising off.

I finally got to Raymond Rosses. Raymond had sort of a dude outfit on Chedsey Creek next to the Forest. I said, "I want to borrow a horse. Any kind of a horse." He lent me one and I rode to Manvilles where the rest of my horses were. I got another horse, took Ray's home, and started looking for tracks along the fences. I found none and stayed all night at Al's.

The next morning I rode back on top and finally followed Jake's tracks. He had gone towards Summit Lake, but some east of it, and had got on a rock ledge that he couldn't get down from. There he was, about a mile from camp! All I can say is, "I learned, even if I learned slow!"

I packed rock salt for the cattle, which was the only kind that was furnished. No two pieces were alike or weighed the same, so I packed lots of rocks around to have a balanced load. Salt was packed in panniers on each side of the horse, so it had to be lifted up and dropped in. Two to three hundred pounds was a load. There were some big salt grounds on top. Sometimes I would leave a packload at one, other times I would leave less. I do not recall salting much down lower when we first went out on the Forest, but the cattle used a lot of salt on top. There was no alkali up there and I could control the cattle movement somewhat by how I salted.

During the summers I would resupply my groceries by pack horse either from Steamboat or from Sid Harris at Hebron. I would try to get to Al Manville's on Monday, Wednesday, or Friday. Those were train nights in Coalmont and generally someone would go down to ship cream (they milked 15 or 20 cows) or get the mail. Occasionally I would get a loaf or two of bread and tie them on behind my saddle wrapped up in my slicker. That was how I'd carry most things, unless there was enough to take a pack horse. Maw Johnson used to make a spice cake in a loaf pan. When she gave me one of those I would live high. I'd tie it on the back of my saddle and head for camp happy!

A man by the name of Keoughan owned the old MacFarlane place that The Big Horn leased. Keoughan was an oilman and had been head honcho of a major oil company or so the story went. Some of Keoughans friends gave him buffalo, three cows and a bull. They never reproduced and when I came all the cows had been disposed of. Only the bull was there.

Frank Hoskinson told me once that he and Bert Wilcox were working calves off cows there one time and the horse Bert was riding was, as many horses were, scared to death of a buffalo. He would bolt and run when that buffalo would as much as peek around the corner of the barn. Bert was working in the gate, letting the cows out and keeping the calves in, so when his horse would sell out it caused quite a mess. Frank added, "Bert cussed the buffalo, cussed Keoughan, and cussed those damn Indians for not killing all the buffalo."

About 1936 it was decided to eliminate the bull buffalo and Frank Hoskinson did the deed. He told me "I'd give people a big piece and they would take it home, cut off a piece, try to eat it, and bring the rest back! I never could give it all away!" The buffalo hide hung over the rafters in the Keoughan barn for years and the wool kept falling down as its grease burned off.

When he was visiting in the late 30's Celly mentioned that he would like to have a buffalo skull. In fact he mentioned that he would buy me a radio for my camp if I could come up with a buffalo skull. I had seen a couple different skulls out in the park in earlier years, but that fall when I looked for them, they were gone. I did know where they had thrown that bull's skull at the Keoughan ranch, so I gathered up that skull and took it to Denver at Stock Show time.

Celly bought me a battery operated radio for about $24 and I enjoyed it at camp and in bunkhouses. It was not only battery operated, but it could be plugged in too.

Celly and I kept track of each other until he passed away. He was as great a friend as I ever had.

Buffalo Pass had been the road from North Park to Steamboat Springs from the start. About 1921 the road over Rabbit Ears Pass was built and not much work was done on Buffalo Pass from then on. It was steep on the North Park side and badly washed. The west side was not as steep but had not been maintained. In fact on top there were still corduroy stretches, (logs laid crossways) that were still in use in the 30's for cars and wagons to cross bogs. It wasn't exactly an automobile road, but cars did get up there, altho' more from the Steamboat side than our side.

I did not know my wife Grace when I was riding the top in the 1930's. We came close to meeting tho' when they made a trip up Buffalo Pass one Sunday by car, or maybe it was pickup, and had lots of trouble. When they got home, Grace's dad, Carlos, discovered he had lost his billfold. They went back the next morning and discovered horse tracks down the road. They went on up and found the billfold near the top. I had come off the top but I had left it up to the horse to keep on the road. I'd see what went on off the road and didn't pay much attention to what was on the road.

I met an assortment of people up there. One time I was down at Longs Lake (where our allotment and The Big Horns met) and there was a pack outfit there. They invited me to lunch there at a picnic table. When we sat down to eat, there was a preacher among them. As I bowed my head while he said the blessing, I got to thinking what if Bill Angel rode up? He was a tease and nobody I could recall said grace at meals. I might have been accused of "getting religion!"

Another group that I stumbled onto was the girls from Perry Mansfield Camp in Strawberry Park. There would be 10 to 15 girls horseback, with a pack outfit. That is where I met Bob Perry whose aunt was one of the founders. Bob handled the pack outfit. They would come out on top and go north. Where they camped I never knew. I would ride along with them for a couple miles, and answer questions about what I was supposed to be doing. And no, I was not lonesome. As I recall they were like 12 to 15 years old.

People going north on the Continental Divide trail could see my camp across the head of the canyon. Those going south never saw it.

One afternoon a white headed man walked in who turned out to be Logan Crawford whose family had been the first settlers of Steamboat Springs. We visited for a couple hours.

I did not have a car but I did buy a horse from a George Woodcock who stopped at my camp for lunch. He told me about this palomino he had. He and I rode to Steamboat and he took me up Elk River to his ranch. There I dealt probably $50 for the horse. I took the horse to camp and he never left from up there. But then I wintered at Johnsons. Early the next spring the snow had mashed the fences down and old Buck left and went over the top on the crusted snow headed back to Steamboat. Jonney Williams ran a livery stable in Steamboat and his son Billy let me know that they had taken my horse in and took care of him. On the 4th of July I took my saddle over, spent the day, and rode Buck back. By then a lot of the snow was gone.

We got considerable cold weather that winter . It would stay around 40 below for a week or 10 days, probably get to 20 below in the daytime, but there was never any wind during those cold snaps.

I recall one morning—I'm not going to try to tell the temperature—when Frank Hoskinson and I rode from the Rosenbaum Ranch to Henry Donelsons to see some calves we were wintering there. Frank had a sheepskin coat with collar that he tucked his nose behind. We rode in a normal trot and when we got nearly there I happened to look at Frank and saw a patch of frost on his cheek the size of a half dollar. His cheek froze as well as my nose. They were sore and the skin peeled off before they healed. We were not alone tho', that same morning Darrel Harris froze his nose going to the Keoughan from Walden.

Another cold winter I was tending some Big Horn calves at the Home Ranch, using an old fashioned coal and wood tank heater to control the ice on the water tank. Jack White, the manager, went to Stock Show in Denver and came home with a fancy new kerosene tank heater along with a lot of the sales pitch that went with it.

It worked well until one morning when it got cold and the kerosene froze to a mush in the tank but wouldn't move through the line. Back to the old fashioned cast iron heater that used coal and wood!

A Jack White story: Jack drove a Buick and was known as a fast driver. One time he came across Bill Monahan stalled in the Hebron Lane with a model T Ford. Jack stopped and asked Bill, "Do you have a chain?" Bill did and hooked his Model T on. As Bill got into his Ford he said, "Willy, you're in the arms of Jesus now!"

I have already mentioned that no elk wintered in North Park, no deer wintered here either. The elk came over the top on the crusted snow in the Spring. The deer went north and wintered in Wyoming. I saw very few deer on top but there were several big bucks that hung out at the foot of the head wall above Newcomb Park. I would see them from the top, generally 6 or 8 in a bunch. Elk did come out on top some and there were several bunches of 10 to 20 that worked the breaks just east of the top. They went as far down as Sawmill Creek but I never saw them as far down as the fences. The first elk that wintered in North Park were 4 or 5 old bulls that stayed on the south slope above Butler Creek about the winter of 1937 or 38. The first deer that I knew of wintering in North Park were on the Mexican. One fall I rode up there to check on some cattle and there were deer west of Pole Mountain.

One Spring The Big Horn had a man with a team and a wagon fixing fence up Mexican Creek staying at the old Billy McGowan homestead. One of his horses got away and he could not catch it. I was staying at the Home Ranch and was sent out one Sunday to capture the wayward horse. After I got that done I rode north between Mexican Ridge and Pole Mountain then down Pony Creek and visited Lou Krause.

That fall again I was staying at the Home Ranch and got word that there were some cattle up Mexican Creek. I rode up and jumped a bunch of yearlings that were running wild north of the Billy McGowan homestead in the steep hill washouts. I got close enough to see that they had the BT brand and knew that they were Bill Trownsell's. I did not want to get upside down in a drywash while alone, so I left and rode north and again stopped at Lou Krause's. The first thing Lou said to me was, "Do you remember last Spring when you stopped by?" I told him that I did and he told me that that was the last time anyone had been there. Goes to show you that you don't have to be on top of a mountain to be isolated.

When I stopped at Trownsells to tell them about those cattle that was the only time I was in the house or talked to Grace Peterson. She was my Grace's grandmother. We used to ride through the yard in winter when the lane (Hiway 14) was snowed up as we went from the Home Ranch to the Keoughan. That happened several winters while I rode for The Big Horn 1938 thru 1941. I always made my headquarters at the Home Ranch but there was another Big Horn cowboy by the name of Darrel Harris that wintered at the Keoughan.

Darrel was a good roper. We roped calves by the head in the spring when they were small. Darrel threw an overhand loop and would rope a hundred calves without a miss.

We got to practicing roping one Spring in Baker Draw. Between the sagebrush and the soap holes there was a strip that had no brush where there was a bunch of cows and calves. We would cut a calf from the bunch and drive it a ways from the cows, then let it break back, rope it, and practice tying it. We went through this practice three or four times, and those old cows were getting smart. When we were going to move those cows and calves our boss Frank Hoskinson was with us. As soon as we rode into sight there were cows bawling, calves bawling, and the whole bunch headed for the sagebrush. Frank kept saying, "I wonder what is bothering those cattle?" He never got an answer from either of us!

One Sunday Darrel suggested we ride to the Norris Ranch where Ratcliffs lived for Sunday dinner. Maw Freeman asked me if we were going to be home for dinner and I said, "No, we are going to Ratcliffs for dinner." She said, "Good. I am going to have strawberry short cake. I'll wait and have it for supper."

We rode over and during dinner the phone rang, it was Frank, our boss. He said, "You guys gather those cattle this afternoon and I'll bring help and we will brand tomorrow morning." I tried to call Maw Freeman but no luck. That one wire phone line we had was no way reliable. I tried again towards evening with no luck. We stayed and branded the next forenoon.

We ate lunch then mounted to go back to the Home Ranch. Darrel was riding a horse called Spade, as in the Jack of Spades. The rumor was he had been in Frank Tate's spade buckin string. He would buck and Darrel was quite sure he could not ride him. We mounted near the barn where the cattle had stayed out of the wind in the shelter of the barn. The snow had just melted and there was near a foot of sloppy cow manure close by. That was where old Spade came undone and Darrel rode him! To say the least the shit did fly.

We both dreaded facing Maw Freeman when we got to the Home Ranch. Do you suppose that Darrel would go down with me? No way! He stayed in the bunkhouse. I go down and knock on the door, Maw opens the door and says, "Well?" I said, "I know we are in the doghouse, but I couldn't get the phone to work." Then she smiled and said, "Come in and visit. The shortcake didn't go to waste. Foreman White came along and ate it." We sat and visited for like half an hour. Poor Darrel was pacing the floor thinking I was in all kinds of trouble, but all was forgiven.

Another time I rode in and went down to report I'd be there for supper. Maw must have seen me coming, she met me at the door with two biscuits. She asked me, "Aren't these good biscuits?"

"Sure!" I said.

She said, "That Charlie called them sinkers! He asked one of the men to please pass the sinkers!" Then we had a visit and that blew over.

Old Bill Latham turned the ranch over in 1936 to his son Charlie. Charlie was not a cowman, he was a mechanic. He sold the cows. I'm sure it was 1938 that the Forest Service allowed Walt Berquist a hundred and fifty heifers in place of the Latham cattle. These heifers came complete with bulls and were bred on the range.

In the fall of 1940 there had been 18 head of Big Horn cows west of camp along the Steamboat road. I knew they were there and doing fine so I got them out late, rode the country well, and felt I had them all. But after hunting season someone in Steamboat told Frank Hoskinson they had seen 36 head of cattle. By that time I was done gathering the Big Park Association cattle and was up at Clover Valley cow camp Frank sent me and Glen Hozelton to check. We loaded old Spade with a bed roll, some grub and some oats, and went to the cabin on top. We stayed all night there and rode clear down the next morning but found no tracks. We came to camp and had lunch.

We had packed Spade who was tied at the corner of the cabin. A camp robber got in the cabin. I did not want him whitewashing the inside and starving to death in there so I finally bopped him with the broom and tossed him out. He took wing but was not very steady and hit old Spade right behind the ear. Spade exploded bucking as far as the halter rope would let him go, but he never lost anything. I never thought one bird could upset one horse that much!

Carl Erickson was a lot of fun when he came up on top to help gather in the fall. He would get lost in those canyons on the west slope but seemed to enjoy those trips. One time we were riding the slope below Lake Dinosaur tracking through snow when we picked up a set of tracks of a dozen animals. We couldn't tell if they were elk or cattle tracks until we came to elk droppings. We got off our horses and Carl picked up some of the elk berries and said "Oley, those are fresh!"

I said, "Taste them, an elk hunter can tell how fresh they are by tasting them."

Carl studied them a bit then said "Oh Shit! I'm not an elk hunter, you taste them!"

One time we were sleeping together on a three quarter bed and springs, with my bed roll on it so it made for close quarters in bed. Carl woke me up in the night and said "Oley, something is in here!"

I said, "It's probably only a pack rat."

He said "Whatever it is, it tried to get my nose!"

We sorted most of the cattle in the fall at Al Manville's, in a fence corner southeast of the house on a bluff. There were some old prairie dog holes that were never filled up. One time Carl Erickson was sorting and his horse got among those holes. Carl lost the critter back into the bunch. Carl got after his horse and said, "You watch the cow! I could see where we were going!"

One summer Carl Erickson went to Sweden. That fall as we were working cattle Carl would get excited and start talking Swedish. I enjoyed it but never got to understanding it.

Me and the horses with camp packed in the fall.

One time when the cattle were still on Chedsey Creek, I came across one of Carl Erickson's steers that had a broken leg. He had jumped a cow and got a front foot in a forked tree. I was able to get him free so I went to Al Manville's and called Carl that evening. He was to come up the first thing in the morning and we would take a pack horse and butcher the steer.

This was July and daylight came early. It got a little light when Carl drove in. I said, "You really got up early!"

And he said, "Hell! Gus Carlstrom got me up!"

Those Swedes didn't seem to require much sleep. In the fall sometimes Carl Erickson would leave Manvilles with a bunch of his cattle, trail them home some 12 miles, maybe sleep a little, catch a fresh horse, and be back to Manvilles for breakfast ready to gather more cattle.

The horses that Carl furnished me on top were sort of average. That Skeeter mare I had the first couple years scared me. I was riding up south of Al Manville's house, where there had been a ditch break that flooded that boulder strewn hill. We hit a boggy spot way up on that hill that had never been there before. Skeeter got bogged pretty bad and stopped strugglin'. I decided to step off just as she made a lunge and I got a spur caught in the slicker on the back of the saddle. It just held for one jump before it came loose. That was one of the few times I got spooked. I sat right down then and cut my spur straps better than halfway through over the buckles so they would break if I ever got hung up by a spur again.

Another scare I was involved in happened one fall. Bud Earl, who was riding for Berquists, and me were at Kiefers gathering strays. Kiefer did not run on the Forest but next to it so we made a swing through his cattle.

Generally we were treated to a good meal and expected to sort his cattle for him. There was snow on the ground and I was riding The Big Horn horse, Kid. Kid turned quick and as his feet went out from under him I could feel my foot still in the stirrup. I held him down and as he struggled I worked my foot free. Bud was right there and wanted to know if he could help. I told him no and turned Kid loose. Kid jumped up, jumped over me, and kicked. I stayed low and he kicked way over me. When I got up Bud was white as a sheet. It had scared him more to watch it than it had me in the middle of it.

Carl Erickson sent me another horse for one or two summers. Hugo was his name. He was sort of green broke with lots of snort. He couldn't buck but he would try and always bawled when he did. His bark was worse than his bite. Hugo never was much of a saddle horse so I used him as a packhorse some. In the summer of 1940 my aunt and uncle from Denver were coming up to spend a couple days. My grub was getting low so I took a couple horses plus Hugo to pack and went to Hebron and got grub.

My Aunt Rachel and Uncle Jim Starr came to the Ranger Station and we started from there about mid-afternoon. It looked like rain so I was in a hurry. I tied Hugo to the fence, blindfolded him with a gunny sack, and proceeded loading him with grub. When he was loaded he pulled back, broke the halter rope, and went to bawling and bucking in the corral blindfolded. He hit the fence head on and skinned his nose. There was a paper

sack of flour that got punctured. Each time Hugo bucked and hit the ground, a puff of flour came out of the pannier. That would have been funny if I'd had time to enjoy it. Aunt Rachel was worried about Hugo's skinned nose but I could have cut Hugo's throat with a dull knife. One thing was sure, Hugo never left much of a vacancy when he left.

Another Erickson horse was Rusty. I rode Rusty for several years on The Big Horn so I took him on top one summer and hobbled him. He quit the top and went hobbled to the Clover

Valley cow camp some 15 miles away. So I never took him back even tho' he was a good horse. John Chambers told of one time he was running a bunch of horses on Rusty. John got off to close a gate and when he got back on Rusty started to crow hop. John said, "I reached up and spurred him in the shoulder. Hell, he hadn't even started to buck, but when he got done bucking I was on the ground!"

Al Manville and I went to Rock River, Wyoming, and bought some horses from a widow whose husband had been killed by a stallion. It may have been a remount stallion that belonged to the United States Government. The U.S. Remount Service put out stallions for ranchers to use to improve the horse herds and there were several in North Park during the 30's and 40's. The stallions were nearly all thoroughbreds. The Remount Service came into North Park and bought horses for the U.S. Army and paid about $175 a head for the ones that passed. Many did not pass, but they seemed to like half-thoroughbreds.

I never thought I'd ever have occasion to see those remount horses again, but I did. The 87th Regiment had cavalry horses when I first joined the Army in 1942, but they did not seem to be as good a caliber as the ones they bought in North Park.

The horses that Al Manville bought at Rock River were thoroughbred type. He bought one broke horse, one green broke horse, and a 2-year old stud that I recall. Al kept the broke black horse. I drew the green broke bay horse that I named Fritz. I was always mounted when I got him a little more broke. Al eventually sold the black horse to the Remount. These were flatland horses I helped gather out at Rock River and it brought back memories of when I grew up on the dry land. One time Al had a wreck with that black horse. We were riding Whalen Creek when we came to a steep hillside with nothing but a little narrow game trail. I got off to lead my horse and Al made fun of a scaredy cat. I got part way across, heard a commotion, looked back, and saw that old pony hanging onto the trail by his front feet. He tried to get up and over he went. He and Al tumbled several times to the bottom. I was afraid to look, but Al had only one skinned place on one shoulder and he didn't have much meat on his bones to bruise.

Al Manville and I had several wrecks, and near wrecks. One morning in the fall we were riding up on the flats, east and south of his house. He had lots of cattle in that field and we ran across a cow with porcupine quills in her nose, then we saw several more. Al was riding his favorite horse name of Stranger. I'm riding old Hippo. I caught the first cow and missed my dallies so she got away with my rope. Al always tied hard and fast so I got a lot of ribbing about losing my rope. We dequilled that cow. The next was a big brockley faced cow. Al caught her around the big middle (between the front legs) and he had not tightened his cinch so that cow was about to pull his saddle over Stranger's head. Al was a little man with somewhat of a hump back and Stranger was a big high-headed horse. Together that was a sight, him begging for me to come catch that cow, and get him out of a pickle. I did follow him around a bit to enjoy it before I caught the cow. As I look back on it tho', I wonder why we didn't gather those cows with the quills and go to the corral.

Al also had chickens and a chicken house banked with loose hay. The dogs had dug nests back into the hay where they slept year round. One fall just at dusk I saw a skunk. I went to some trouble getting the dogs to see it. They did and triggered what a skunk does. That night Al started to the barn to turn some horses out. A couple of minutes later he came back to the house, lit a coal oil lantern, got his .22 rifle, and said, "There is a skunk in the chicken house." He did not find anything. The next night he went to turn out the horses and the same thing happened, rifle and the works. When he got back that night I asked him, "Have you smelled your dogs lately?" He won some and I won some, but we had lots of fun and a good relationship and re-mained friends for as long as he lived.

We used to trail cattle up from Newcomb Park. The trail went north of Round Mountain Lake a short way, but the cattle did get around the lake. One time we had them nearly all on the

south side of the lake. An old cow who knew where she was going took out up a sort of chute that looked too steep for a cow to go up, but up we went. We used that route from then on. One time we were going up that chute when a couple of bulls got into a fight above me. One got whipped and came down, barely missing me and old Hippo who wasn't geared to move that fast.

Sometimes in Colburn Draw a young bull would get located with a bunch of cows. When I'd go to move them along that narrow forest trail to Beaver Creek then on to Newcomb Park that young bull would get ahead of the cows and fight them back. That, my friends, was not good trailing.

One fall Al and I were at my camp on a still cold morning when we heard cattle bawling. We rode toward the ruckus for a mile or two, then decided that it was The Big Horn moving out of Clover Valley a good ten miles away.

I had some recreation and entertainment on top. There were chipmunks. I had a small pair of binoculars and I used to watch chipmunks peel grains of oats, then stuff the grain into their pouches. There were red foxes that used to hunt mice in the meadow around camp. They would go along, either hear or see something, and they would jump and land where they thought the mouse was, then very carefully lift one foot at a time to see if there was a mouse under it.

There were Camp Robbers, Grey Jays or Whiskey Jacks, all the same bird. They were always around camp. I never bothered them and they got real tame. I used to buy a two-pound box of cheese and along toward fall I was trimming some mold off of it and threw the trimmings out. Lots of Camp Robbers showed up and they were having a grand time, when a mean streak popped out in me. I got a mouse trap, put it on a stump, and baited it with cheese scraps. They would go for the cheese and the trap would scare them away. Finally one old wise bird flew down and hopped all around the trap and tried to go in from the side. The trap hit him along the side of the head and cold cocked him for an instant. He gathered himself up and flew away sort of wobbly. An added note. One winter I skied to Steamboat in February to the Ski Tournament. I stopped near my summer camp sight to eat lunch and a Camp Robber showed up for the scraps.

Another bird that always fascinated me was the Water Ouzel. The only place I ever saw them was down Mad Creek, never

BILL CULBERTSON
© 1994

near the top. They had one loud squawk or chirp or whatever.
They were a dark grey bird and were always along the creek
bank until they would walk right into the water and feed around

on the bottom, chirping all the while. An Ouzel was not the least bit afraid of a person. Quite an attraction for a dry-lander.

I never did figure out how I could be so lucky as to be paid for a job that was so perfect. There was never two days alike. I'd go north one day, south the next day, and see something new every day, like weather. If it was cloudy and I could see under the clouds west toward sundown, it would be fair the next day.

Lightning was something else. There would be tremendous lightning storms, even static electricity so potent I've seen the sparks jump between a horse's ears when he shook his head. And after a violent lightning storm I would find a tree literally shattered, sometimes as far down as the stump, with splinters some as big as 2x6's. There was a dead tree on the Stillwater that was struck about every other summer while I was up there. The wood grain went around the tree. When the lightning struck it there would be a strip several inches wide taken off from near the top to the bottom and new wood would show through. Then when that got weathered in a year or two, a new strip would appear. Never but once did I see where lightning had struck a Quaker tree.

One evening just about sundown I saw a perfectly round rainbow south and east of my camp in the head of the canyon. Oh, how I wished for a color camera then! But there were none for many years after that.

My mom came and visited me in the summer of 1940. She stayed several days, then told me that finally she could understand how I could spend my time up there alone and be satisfied. It may have helped that we had perfect weather while she was there. There was something special about the greenness of the grass that is hard to explain. Could be the sunshine at 10,500 feet?

My mom wanted me to quit chewing tobacco and when I went out home one fall she presented me with a pound can of Sir Walter Raleigh smoking tobacco and a pipe, with instruc-

My mom at my cabin in 1940.

tions to quit chewing! I tried smoking. I never carried the pipe, but would smoke it some in the evening. I kept a part of a plug of chewing tobacco in my pocket all winter and never took it out until I went back to cowboying in the spring.

How did I come to chew tobacco? When I was growing up I was a friend of old Charley Ladall. He and I trapped some and never caught much, but we were friends. He told me one time "If when you reach 21 and won't use tobacco I will give you a hundred dollars." But when I got to be 21 in the fall of 1932 nobody had a hundred dollars. I was riding colts in the spring of 1932 and a cold wind kept blowing. I had a couple of teeth that were ouchy and I found that by putting a wad of chewing tobacco on it helped. The next thing I knew the weather had warmed up and I was still chewing tobacco. I chewed only tobacco until the summer of 1936 when my brother Dutch, who was working for Turpens at the time, came up to my camp looking for an elk. We didn't do any good but he had a can of snuff along. I tried it and became a snoose chewer for 16 years.

In the winter we Big Horn cowboys didn't have a very strenuous schedule. Some days we never saddled up a horse. Hank McDaniels used to say, "Today leave us blow the stink off." That meant let's ride somewhere. We didn't have medicine as they have today, so we never doctored many cows, but we did ride around and look. If we were out when it was real cold we would stop and ask the poor guy that was pitching the hay if he had a guest fork. And maybe we would help with a load of hay to warm us up. One time Maw Freeman was to go to Laramie to get her hair done, she asked me if I would set the dinner on for Charlie and the boys at noon. I said I would and we had dinner without a hitch. But it got towards supper time and no Maw. Hank was there. He and I went down to rustle up some supper. We found everything we needed but bread so we baked a batch of biscuits and they didn't turn out too bad. About the time supper was over Maw arrived. She never got over the fact that we could bake a batch of biscuits!

Maw Freeman was a good cook. That was in the depression days when people were out trying to find any kind of a job. Freemans hired a couple from Arkansas or Missouri. Anyway Maw coddled eggs, put them in boiling water and then set them back for so many minutes producing a soft boiled egg. This one morning Maw came out while this farm woman was getting breakfast. The eggs were on the front of the cook stove boiling away. Maw said, "Charlie and the boys don't like their eggs hard boiled!" The cook looked at her and said, "WE like them!"

One Fall Frank Hoskinson and I came down to the Home Ranch for the first time since Spring with a bunch of cattle. It was the first of November. How well I recall Jim Peterson being there for lunch and telling of the hell that been raised in Walden the night before. I said, "Jim, you know that you did worse than that!"

He said, "Did I ever tell you about the time we put the milk cow in the church?" Seems they put the cow in the church on Friday night and had furnished her with a bale of hay and a tub of water. The cow did all right, but nobody milked her and her bag spoiled by the time she was discovered on Sunday morning.

After hearing that story I pulled a great big boo-boo. I told you Maw Freeman was a darn good cook. She made the most beautiful pies ever, but the filling tended to be dry and if she put cinnamon in it, it was just a dash in the bottom. This day for lunch we had cherry pie and was it ever good! When I had finished lunch Maw asked me, "How did you like the pie?" I said, "Great! The best pie you ever made!" She said, "Well! I like that! Bess Peterson made it!" When we got back to the bunkhouse Frank said, "You can open your mouth bigger than anybody of your size that I ever saw!"

Speaking of pies. One time I came down off the top to Al Manville's and the cooks had gone back to Kansas for a visit. There were several men there and I volunteered to get supper. As I scrounged the pantry I found some apples and decided to make a pie. I had not made a pie for years and when I mixed the crust it didn't look like pie crust, it reminded me of rawhide but I went ahead and made the pie anyway. The crust turned out tough and way above the apples. I was not going to serve it, but as we were setting down to supper the cook came home and served that pie, and it was eaten! Those guys must have been pie hungry!

One spring I was staying at Johnsons when Al came up and wanted to know if I could help him. It was spring and I thought that he was going to brand calves so I went with him. When we got there he was alone and batching, and milking some 15 or

20 cows! He wanted me to help him clean some ditches down in that bog. So we settled in to milking the cows, separating the cream off, doing the dishes, washing the separator, batching, and ditching with a 4-horse team on a wing plow and a Martin Ditcher. Most days we never stopped for lunch altho' we would be less than a mile from the house. We were putting in mighty long days and I would be sleeping in a morning when Al would come in and twist my ears to awaken me. I did not appreciate this. One evening Al said, "If you will do the dishes, I'll go to Coalmont to ship cream and get the mail."

As I was doing the dishes I had a bright idea. We had many gallon cans that fruit and veggies came in and we used them when separating to catch the cream. I took about 15 of these cans into my bedroom and made a pyramid in front of the door. The next morning when Al got up I heard him start for the kitchen, then remember me. He turned around and hit that door running. No more ear twisting!

All cattle were shipped by rail in the 30's. We would leave Manvilles before noon and trail to Hebron slow. We would get to the railroad stockyards around sundown with the cattle partly full, and leave them in the yards all night. The train stayed in Coalmont all night, leaving there at 6 am, arriving at Hebron around 6:30. As the cattle cars were loaded, the train crew would spot the next car to be loaded.

One Fall Al and I trailed his cattle down to Hebron, just got them yarded at dusk, and had to ride the 10 or 12 miles home. As we left the yards Al said, "I'll have to get up and come down and car these cattle in the morning."

I said, "I'll help you," to which he replied, "You can't get up in the morning!"

It so happened I was sleeping in the garage and the next morning the coyotes howled and the dogs barked and woke me up. I looked at my watch and saw it was 4 o'clock. I jumped out of bed, got dressed, went into the house, pulled the covers off Al and said, "Let's go car those cattle!" He jumped up, got

dressed, and we got into his pickup and to Hebron we went. There was no heater that worked in said pickup and it was cold that October morning. Finally Al turned on a light and discovered that we still had over an hour to wait for the train. Then was when I told him, "Never tell me I can't get up in the morning!"

Before I rode for The Big Horn, they were shipping a train load of cattle, dry cows and yearling steers. Jack White, the manager, told the cowboys, "There won't be any hurry in the morning."

It is a bit over a mile from the Home Ranch to the Hebron stockyards. Jack White got there early, got cold and climbed up into the locomotive where it was warm, and got to wondering where the cowboys were. Finally he had the bright idea that if he blew the whistle they would come! He blew it just once as the south side of the Hebron stockyards was mashed out by all the cattle leaving.

It was 9 o'clock that night before they got them all caught and loaded. After that, the railroad rebuilt the Hebron stockyards and they were in good shape when I helped load cattle there.

Another time Al sold his yearling steers to old Vic Hanson who was the brand inspector. They worked them and we started to Hebron with them. In the first couple of miles I had found 3 stray steers in the bunch, they took them out, but I wondered.

They told me a tale from the year before I rode the top. Young Bill Latham was helping trail cattle when they got to the Butler School. It was recess and young Bill rode up and told the kids to get the hell out of sight. They went into the horse barn that stood just south of the gate the cattle were to go through. There was a manure window by that corner and when the cattle were just about to go through the gate, one of the Norrell boys stuck his hat out the window and waved it. They never did get those yearlings through that gate. They had to take them almost a mile north to another gate and come down the road just past the school.

Norells contracted the School Section then. The boys Bud and Buss rode horseback to school. School then was a summer school that started in about April and lasted until it snowed up, generally about Thanksgiving. One time when I was at the School Section for lunch Dewey Norell took his fly rod and we went to the creek in the corral. He caught a mess of trout in about half an hour and we had a great lunch. Norells leased the Staples Place from Pattersons. Mrs. Patterson was Frank Staple's daughter.

Charles Freeman was "Scharley "to Katy "Maw" Freeman. She was German and I believe came from there and so talked with some accent. As my dad came from Germany I had no trouble understanding her.

Rumor had it that she was older than Charley who was an ex-prize fighter and one of the hardest working men I ever knew. He was forever trying to find a way to load hay other than with a pitchfork. They tried using a needle, a long steel rod threaded to a cable that was pushed through the stack and pulled through. This done, they took a hitched team to try and pull the hay onto the sled. They also tried cabling the hay onto the sled by going around the stack and pulling it onto the sled, but none of these worked very well. The snow generally was drifted around the stacks and the men and teams were working in a lot of snow. Charley ran a good feeding operation in winter tho' and they fed with three 4-horse teams, changing horses every day. They'd leave the today's team in the barn overnight and catch fresh horses before daylight. They used a lot of horses and had a horse lot back of the barn where they always fed lots of hay.

Some winters there were lots of jack rabbits. I used to take a box of shotgun shells and hunt afoot until the shells were gone. Then I'd saddle up a horse to gather the rabbits and hang them over the saddle horn because jackrabbits were worth maybe a dime apiece.

Billy McGowan contracted the Keoughan ranch, and was helped by Vern Adams who was the top hay pitcher on The Big Horn. In my estimation, he was one guy that didn't need any help.

I always liked to stay at McGowans. On occasion I went to the Coalmont mine to get a load of coal for the bunkhouse. I'd be ready to go as soon as lunch was over, drive to the pit with a team and sled, and load up and get home about dark. One trip I'll never forget started at McGowans. I was there at noon on a below zero day with Darrel Harris when the boss called up and said, "Go to the Buffalo ranch, there are some dry cows there." We saddled up and I remember I rode old Spot. We went to Joe Coyte's east of Seymores and they told us how to get to the Dennis Brennen place where there would be a trail to the Buffalo ranch. From there there was about 2 feet of snow and we got to the Buffalo ranch just at sundown. The guy in charge came out and we told him what our mission was. He pointed down the creek, said, "The feed ground is down there," turned around, and went back into the house. We made a quick sweep through the feed ground found maybe a dozen Big Horn cows before it got dark. We broke trail out to the cutoff road and then had to break trail back west to Coyte's. We had some kind of a trail back to the Keoughans. When we got there about 10:30 at night it was 32 below zero.

Frank Hoskinson called up and said Vic Hanson had run some steers up on the Mexican and was out 6 or 7 steers and asked would I furnish him a horse and go with him the day after Christmas to try to find those steers. It turned out to be another below zero day. Vic showed up with no chaps, his bony knees sticking out in the breeze. We got mounted and took out. After we had passed Coalmont I said, "Let us get off and walk."

Vic said "We ain't got time."

I thought to myself, "I'll just freeze that old bastard solid!" We rode up Mexican Creek around back of Pole Mountain, finally came out at Turpens, rode the feed ground there, and found all the steers.

After we got them started down the lane, I said "I'll ride ahead and trot over to Coalmont and get my mail." When I met Vic at the Y north of Coalmont he said, "I been thinking of going to Old Mexico...I'm going!" Vic froze his hands that day and never took a wintertime ride with me again.

Most years that I rode on top I helped The Big Horn gather in the fall, after the Association cattle were all gathered. It was in the fall of 1935 that I was sent to Clover Valley cow camp to meet Ordway Mellen. We stayed all night, then saddled up and headed for Steamboat Valley to ride fields for North Park strays. I rode a good black mare of The Big Horns. Ordway rode a big bay horse of his own. The day we started it was snowing and we went up where Hiway 40 had been oiled that year. There was snow on the oil and Ordway's horse fell in the first hundred yards. I thought it was funny until my horse fell about 500 yards later. Then Ordway thought it was funny too!

We stopped at Columbine and I got a new pair of sunglasses. Cars were still getting across the pass and we pulled some back on the road with our saddle horses. We arrived at Bill Werners for supper and stayed there while we rode the fields. In the lane where the Oak Creek road turns off 40, we picked up a couple of steers that somebody told us had a ZV brand.

We caught one of those steers. He had been picked with a knife, but not clipped. They had picked the 7 down and connected it with the bar to come up with a Z. They were 7V's, Carl Erickson's, my charges from Buffalo Pass. In all we got 29 head of North Park cattle for 5 or 6 owners, then on the 5th of November we moved to Val Brunners at the foot of Rabbit Ears Pass to be in position to leave to cross the mountains. That was my birthday and Mary Brunner had a birthday cake for me. The next morning it was still snowing. We got up at 3 am and had breakfast as Mrs. Brunner fixed us a lunch. We saddled up in front of the barn where they had a light (they had a light plant). I tied my lunch on the back of my saddle while Ordway mounted. After I had mounted I took a chew then I offered the plug to Ordway. He looked all around and said, "I might consider matrimony this morning, but I wouldn't consider a chew." We were up past the Spud Patch by the time it got light and that is where we hit the highway. There were no tracks and the pass was closed. We made it to the road camp to eat our lunch. One shed was not locked so we got in out of the snow but there was no heat. Ordway was riding a big horse, some 17 hands high so he did most of the trail breaking. The snow was stirrup deep but light. That evening we got to the old summit around dark when it quit snowing and the moon came out. As soon as we got on a down slope we left the cattle and rode to the Clover Valley cow camp. The snow was too deep to do any trotting. It must have been past 8 pm when we got there. A cold camp and a long day.

Ordway Mellen and I made many a trip to Pleasant Valley at the foot of Rabbit Ears Pass in the fall to gather cattle. Those ranchers ran up on Storm Mountain and Walton Creek. Ordway ran south and west of Rabbit Ears peak so he mixed as well with The Big Horn that ran north and west of Rabbit Ears peak. One fall we went to Middle Park and rode the Sam Martin fields. Ordway got one bull that trip. We stayed one night in that big old log house of Sam Martin's and slept upstairs. There was no heat and the wind was blowing. I got right into bed, Ordway was slow undressing and said, "There for sure ain't any willows in here to get behind." But we slept warm. As was the custom then there were about 5 or 6 quilts on the bed. I enjoyed the visit that we had with Sam Martin that trip. He was the first settler on Muddy Creek. He told us that he had came way up the creek to settle because the hunting had been better.

Ordway Mellen had been born in North Park in 1895 and still lived on the same ranch when I was there. It was a pleasure to ride with him. He never married until about 1940, and we enjoyed bachelorhood together.

One fall there was a Big Horn cow, a brockley faced, half Shorthorn with her calf that got into the Turner meadow. Somebody showed up afoot and the cow jumped the buckfence and came on down the country, leaving the calf there.

Before it snowed I had spotted a Big Horn cow in Latham's west of the Newcomb Creek bridge, south of the Butler School House. She seemed to be a dry cow and wild! I popped brush for some time and never got her out in the open but once or twice, then I gave up. After it had snowed I heard of a bum calf up at Turners so I went up and got it. As I came back with the calf I saw the Chedsey brothers feeding hay across from the Latham gate. I rode in and soon found the wild cow and got her on the road. She traveled much faster than the calf and got way ahead by the time we dropped down Pound Hill. I saw the gate open into the Staples pasture. There was no road or bridge then, only a couple of wagon tracks across the sagebrush. The wild

cow turned in and headed for the willows. Me and this brown horse I was riding got on the wagon track and were making a run to try to head her off from the willows when suddenly I remembered there was a hole between the tracks. At about that moment Brownie ran into that hole with both front legs, and we had a wreck. He turned ass over tincup! I got free but as he came over, the cantle of the saddle connected with my instep.

Remember there was a foot or more of snow so it made for a nice fall. I got up on one leg and Brownie got up on three. We never saw that cow again that day. It wasn't too far to the School Section where I had another horse. I changed horses and took the bum calf to the Home Ranch where he was paired up and he sucked.

John Chambers showed up and I said one day, "Let us catch our best rope horses and go up to the Staples pasture and if we have to, we'll rope that wild cow and bring her down here."

We rode up there, and when we saw that wild cow in the edge of the willows she came right out down the lane and into the bunch. I never saw her again to know her.

John Chambers had ridden for The Big Horn in the late 20's or early 30's then came back and rode for several years in the late 30's. He had a small ranch above Hayden and the White Ranch. He was a good hand who never gave out and was always there at the end of the trail. John could be lots of fun even tho' he liked to bitch about the horses that he rode. One expression he had was, "I'd rather walk, carry my saddle, and drag a chunk than ride that no good son-of-a-bitch!"

John once told me a story about a short cowboy with an even shorter temper. He was riding lanes over on Bear River in the Hayden area, gathering cattle out of the lanes and pushing them back onto the free range and sagebrush. One time he had a small bunch of cattle when he came to the bridge across the river. There was a fisherman sitting on the bridge. Shorty rode up and asked him if he would move until he had crossed the cattle. He rode back, gathered cattle, and waited, and waited. Finally he tried to charge the cattle by and lost them all. John said, "He jerked down his rope, loped up, and whipped that dude across the withers and jumped him off into the river!"

Probably in the fall of 1938 I came down from on top in September to Al Manvilles where I met Harry Wattenburg and Vic Carlstrom. They had come to spend the night because they were to receive a bunch of purebred Hereford heifers that Gus

Carlstrom had bought from Ferrington Carpenter of Hayden. They were to meet them on top of Buffalo Pass at noon the next day, so I went with them. We rode leisurely to my camp, I got us some lunch, and then we waited…and waited. Finally we started down the western slope and found them several miles from the top with a tired sore footed bunch of cattle. As near as I can recall there were 60 or 70 head that we took over. We got on top just at dark. We could see the cattle pretty well in the pine timber where the white faces showed up. Then when we got into the quaker timber we could see the red bodies as we got past the old Bennet and Wells sawmill where there was a fence that was partly down. Harry Wattenburg was riding a horse that was afraid of wire and I'll never forget how the sparks flew when he got tangled up in that wire but his horse never got a scratch. We encountered range cattle before we got to the Little Grizzly Station. There was a good corral there so we left them. As I recall it was 10 pm when we got to Al's. The next morning we had plenty of cattle but not all the right ones. There was several of those heifers missing! We gathered most of them that fall, but one went down the Fish Creek Trail and two went back to Strawberry Park at the foot of Buffalo Pass on the west.

In the summer of 1940 I rode for Carl Erickson and Al Manville. We did not push any cattle up on top but some old cows went up anyway, just enough to be a pain to look after.

That year The Big Horn sold 700 two year old heifers for feeders at $37 a head and offered to sell cows at $55 a head.

There were two immense men that came from Iowa interested in buying 150 Shorthorn Cows. We referred to them as the beef trust. Neither of them would get on a horse, they stood up in the back of the pickup at The Rosenbaum Ranch as we held the bunch. Frank Hoskinson would cut a cow out and they would take her or turn her down. We sorted 150 cows that way! The cows were to be shipped to Iowa so they had to be tested for brucellosis. When we tested them there were 77 reactors!

Jack White, the Big Horn manager said "That has to be

wrong!" So we tested them again. Those Shorthorn cows were not happy being run through that chute again and they protested to the extent that there was very little of the corrals or chute left when we got done. We got 78 reactors that time and that was the end of that sale!

Cattle went up considerably that year. I recall Blunt Simson paid $99 a pair for good young cows with calves in the Spring of 1941.

We did ship a lot of cattle tho', mostly from Walden by railroad. The winter before we had 150 dry cows the Big Horn wanted to send to the Loveland Sugar factory to be fattened. The Big Horn had an arrangement with The Great Western Sugar Company (which Mr. Boettcher owned), whereby they used the sugar company's feed lots, first at Scotts Bluff, Nebraska, then at Loveland Colorado.

A Mrs. Greeley was in the trucking business and took the job of hauling them there. The cows were at the Home Ranch and I helped load them. As I recall the truck was a straight truck that held about 15 cows. The endgate was not fancy. It was set in the corral and had to be carried up the chute and put in after the cows were in the truck. How well I remember the last load! Naturally the wild cows kept getting back and that last load was wild and snotty! Mrs. Greeley had a young man helping her and after many trips up and down the chute the cows were all in the truck. This fellow started up with the end gate when those wild cows decided to come down the chute. I never saw such a wreck, every one of them jumped over that fellow! He must have had some kind of luck because he came away without a scratch.

That was also the spring that the south end sold. Blunt Simson, together with a partner name of Russell, bought the Home Ranch. The Big Horn decided to move the Freemans to the Boettcher Ranch. So what in effect happened was that Maggie Simson and Maw Freeman traded houses.

Hank McDaniels and I were staying at the Home Ranch

and we had an old Dodge pickup that belonged to the company. We used it to help move when we were not busy cowboying. We would take a load from the Home Ranch to the Boettcher Ranch, then bring back a load for Simsons.

Both of those women were good housekeepers and it was amusing to hear the same story at both ends of the haul: "I'm leaving a clean house and moving into a dirty one!" It was all in the eye of the beholder.

In the fall of 1941, after I had finished gathering cattle, I started trapping. I had a Ford car that I had bought in 1940 from Carlos Case. I bought the car from Dave Eaton who was salesman for them. So I was running quite a long trapline by car. I had coyote sets both at Johnson's upper place and at Al Manville's. Al had some Kansas guys working there and although I would never skin a skunk one of these guys would for $2 each. When I'd catch a skunk I would tie it onto the bumper and take it to him. I must have caught 8 or 10 that year and their pelts brought $4 or $5 apiece.

I was staying at Johnson's School Section and helping bale hay when I wasn't trapping. That fall I trapped Pole Mountain Lake for muskrats. I must have caught near a hundred and I gave Elmer Brinker half.

I was trapping Pole Mountain Lake when Pearl Harbor happened. Glen Weatherwax and I had been out the night before and were still asleep when Neva Brown came and woke us up and told us. Glen had been in the army for a year and a day. So he was called right back while I waited for the draft board to call me up.

I did help Carl Erickson with showing a couple loads of cattle at Stock Show in Denver in January of '42. Before I left I checked with the draft board and told them I was going to Washington State to visit my mother. They thought I should have a preliminary physical before I left so I helped load the cattle and went to Dr. Cunningham. He was out in the country

Me around trapping time before I got my hair cut.

and I waited until near sundown when he got back. I think it was in the courtroom in the court house where he had me take off all my clothes. He picked up one foot then the other and said, "You're not flatfooted!" After the "physical" I had to drive to Denver in a snowstorm.

After Stock Show I went out to Groswolds Ski factory. There was the first that I heard of the Ski Troops. Thor told me, "They are going to have a lot of good equipment!" But he never told me I was going to have to carry it all on my back. When I asked how to get into the Ski Troops, Thor Groswold said, "I'll put you in!" I later learned he was the head of the National Ski Patrol west of the Mississippi. I also didn't know about those three letters of recommendation he sent until after I was in. I drove to the state of Washington and in due time was called up for service in the United States Army thereby ending another chapter of my life and starting still another entirely new experience.

"Go outside and holler! Maybe Oley can hear you then!"

> — *Eva Wattenberg to Harry Wattenberg as a comment on the reliability of The Big Horn's one-line phone system*

After the War

In the Army we use to sit around a fire (not in the front) and discuss what we were going to do after the war. I said "I'm not going to disturb any more cows!" After I got discharged November 14th, 1935, I went to Washington State and looked into the propane gas business. In Denver I checked out the insurance business. In January I called The Big Horn. The Big Horn was at that time managed by Waldo Axelson who I'd known most of my Big Horn Days. Was Waldo ever glad to hear from me! He hired me over the phone as cow foreman at $125 a month. I made a trip to Washington State and returned to go to work about the 3rd or 4th of February 1946.

I had shipped my saddle and bed roll from Washington. As I had disposed of my Ford car during the war, again I was afoot, so I rode the bus to Ft. Collins. There I met Billy McGowan who brought me to North Park and delivered me to the Hanson Ranch by Cowdrey where The Big Horn headquarters were.

I moved into the Hanson Ranch bunkhouse. It did not have running water and the necessary place was out north, shared with the people in the cookhouse. They were a young couple from New York State, by the name of John and Frances Springstead, who with Waldo and Pauline Axelson, the manager, were the permanent inhabitants on the Hanson Ranch. The Big Horn had acquired the Hunter Ranch east of the Hanson Ranch and John McCasland was there. Howard and Ethel Hamilton and girls were on the Hill Ranch. Wayne and Alice Geer and boys were on the Shafer Ranch, and Gus McDaniels and his brother were on the Boettcher Ranch. Lake Creek was not occupied in winter but we had a cow camp there each summer.

In 1946, The Big Horn had 2,100 Hereford cows and heifers. They always kept 300 heifers that were exposed to the bulls as yearlings, but being short-aged were never anywhere near all bred. The bulls, it goes without saying, were Herefords and there were 85 to 90 of them. There were 300 or more horses, with a half-Thoroughbred half-Morgan stud and a Belgian stud. I might add here there were *NO* tractors on the outfit. Except for light plants and one old Dodge pickup, The Big Horn owned nothing that consumed gasoline.

There were a number of 4-year-old unbroken half Thoroughbred horses, as well as all ages of draft horses. There were five hay crews that used all horses. It seemed every one wanted broke horses and not too many were breaking colts to work. It was the same way with milk cows. Everyone wanted a milk cow or two, but not many were being broke to milk. There were a few Shorthorn cows scattered about, and we soon bought a Shorthorn bull to upgrade the milk cows.

The first-calf heifers were on the Perkins place north across the road from the Hanson Ranch. The cow herd was generally in bunches of 400 around on the ranches. We did make a habit of wintering the 300 heifer calves on the Hunter Ranch. The bulls were wintered on the Hanson Ranch and summered in the bull pasture on the Shafer Ranch the same as it had been done in the 30's. It still had as many bogs, willows, and beaver dams as it had before too!

One gathered that the help obtainable during the war had left a lot to be desired. Waldo said that they were short 150 some cows the year before. Whether they were gone or if they had been stolen was never decided. There were a number of us who were secretly made deputy sheriffs for several years, but I never felt that there was any rustling that went on. I might say here I generally never had but about five cows a year that I didn't have in my books the years I was cow foreman.

One spring while Chuck Gavin was ranch foreman on the Hanson Ranch, I was over in the Perkins place where I was calving heifers. Chuck and I met along the south fence of the Perkins. It was a buckfence, not too high, and Chuck mentioned that fence needed to be raised up. I said "Leave it alone. This way I can jump Old Blue over it and not have to ride to a gate."

Chuck said, "You never saw the day that horse could jump that fence!" Really I had never jumped Old Blue. I got back and made a run and jumped the fence. I had not looked at where we were to land! It was muddy, and Old Blue's legs bogged. He stopped right there, and my momentum carried me right over his head. I skidded on that gravel road on my elbows and knees, and every pebble took a strip of hide, which goes to show, look before you leap!

In the spring of 1946 Waldo hired a ranch foreman, one Charles Gavin. He and his wife Shirley and a son Mike moved into the small log house across west of the Platte, where Waldo and Pauline had lived the many years Waldo was ranch foreman. That was the setup when calving season came. Those 300 two-year old heifers were in the Perkins place that was rented. In those days there was no pregnancy testing done, so we kept all the heifers underfoot until they quit calving. As I was the entire cow outfit, I calved the first-calf heifers. I had 2 calving chains and the first calf-puller I had ever seen. There was an old log barn with 2 stalls where I could keep a heifer in. I had to carry water, and the hay had been dropped off by whoever did the feeding. Mostly I heeled the heifer, pulled the calf and got away from there before she got up, otherwise she may get up and quit the country and never know that she had become a mother. Any problem birth I would take to the barn. I never looked at them at night. I'd see them by the last light and be there at first light. When I got a moment I would try to see a bunch of cows, but mostly they calved on their own, and did surprisingly well. They were used to being on their own.

I found several horses left that I knew. Jake, Ike, Silver, Ugly and Vinegar were some I recall, as well as Pedro and Tommy that Hank McDaniels had broke. There were several new horses, in particular a blue horse that had been soured. I suffered with him until I got so I could stop him then I rode him many a mile. Remember there were no horse trailers and no trucks.

In 1946 this is how I found The Big Horn and how it operated. Waldo and I were the best of friends, and I was considered second in command when he was gone. Waldo's way of doing business was that we are not a big outfit so we are going to be neighbors. That cost some through the years but I always had a good feeling about my years there under Waldo Axelson. He was as fair a man as I ever dealt with.

On a normal day after breakfast I would go over to the big house where Waldo and I would talk over the day's work. There was no TV then, but there was radio. I recall one morning in 1948 when the Olympics were on and it was reported that many of the Olympic Flags were missing. I said, "I know who took them!"

Pauline questioned how in the world I could know anything about that? My answer was, "Fred Fortune is there sliding bobsleds, and the flags are missing."

Fred Fortune and I met during the war and spent our combat days in the Army together. He as jeep driver and me as supply man. We had many a close call together and I still feel that he saved my life while we were on Kiska. Between jokes and stories Fred told me that he had been a bobsled racer before the war. After the war Fred and his bobsled made it to the Olympics and won a medal there. When I asked Fred about those flags many years later he said, "You were right!"

Frances Springstead was the cook, and her husband Johnny was chore boy at the Hanson Ranch. Johnny milked the cows, and cleaned the barns, since there was a stud or two that was kept in. One chore was not a small item. He carried water from the pump house for the cookhouse and he also fed in an emergency. Emergencies were frequent in those days right after the War. Mostly, ranch hands consisted of winos from Larimer Street in Denver. There were a few ranch hands that were not winos, but generally all hay hands were.

In spring of 1946 Waldo bought a jeep. It was new, and may have been an Army jeep. It was the right color. He tried it out and told me one day, "That jeep can do everything but climb a tree." Until one day he got stuck in Trappers Draw and had to walk to the Hill Ranch. But it *was* a lot of help. I could drive to those west side ranches, catch a horse and get some cows looked at instead of riding 10 or 15 miles to get there.

By the time winter feeding was done most of the cows from the Shafer Ranch were turned into the Boettcher Ranch, and then the gates in the Gap were opened. Those cattle drifted out through Lake Creek to the open range. Some of it was school land and some BLM land on the flats between the Hill Ranch and the west side of the Hanson Ranch, over Independence Mountain to the Wyoming line north and the Platte lane south, (there was a cattle guard on the Ridge Road there). The two year olds we took to the Hill Ranch and when we could go on to the Forest, (July 1st), they would be taken over the Hog Back to Helena Valley.

The Big Horn ran no horses on the open range anywhere after I came back. The excess horse herd was wintered in the upper DeWeese meadow north and west of the bull pasture on the Shafer Ranch, then turned out on the Hog Back when the hay gave out, generally in March. That became a chore I did every spring. I'd take a strong horse and break a track across to the Hog Back and move those horses, generally 150 to 200, onto the Hog Back where there was no water. They ate snow for water. They had come off a good ration of hay and had a water hole available all winter. They would pick up out on that strong feed that grew on the west side of the Hog Back that was swept bare by those ever-present winds.

The draft mares with colts were kept separate and put into the Sandhouse homestead northwest of the Hill Ranch and the Belgium stud turned in with them around the first of July. The saddle mares were kept around the Hanson Ranch and bred in smaller pastures there.

Mostly the cows and calves that went onto the Forest were branded at the Hill Ranch and drifted over the Hog Back to Helena valley and distributed from there. We did build a small corral on the old Peral road south of the Swede Mile at the lower end of Trotman Draw where we branded small bunches and put them on the forest there. To get cattle on Line Creek, we would work off the dry 2-year olds that did not breed the first year and make up around 100 head. We would take them as the road to Hog Park goes now through Pearl, then work them south, and take the bulls to go with them from the Shafer Ranch past Big Creek Lake and through Tisty Park and over Beaver Creek to Line Creek.

Each year I would move to Lake Creek along in June and have a cow camp there for the summer. I would have to change my address from Cowdrey to Walden as the mail route came to the Boettcher ranch. Then in the fall I'd change it back. It was no big deal.

When it came time to move to Lake Creek in 1946, Waldo decided to move the Springsteads there for the summer. Their possessions were loaded on a hayrack pulled by a team. That took them to the south side of the lake at Lake Creek, where they got into some muddy ground and the team quit. The horses wouldn't pull any farther, so they walked and carried bedding and food for the night. They gave us a call, and we sent a team that would pull so they could get their belongings to the build-ings and set up housekeeping. Johnny rode some, fixed fence some, and irrigated. We tried to keep another man there, but I do not recall anyone that summer of 1946.

The Lake Creek buildings from left to right: the shop, backhouse, barn, bunkhouse, and the house.

I did have a bad day that spring when I went to scatter salt on the Forest. I left the Boettcher Ranch and went to the Old Lodge where Waldo had left some salt to be packed and scattered on the Forest. I took two pack horses, Vinegar and a black horse that had to be called Shit-Head. We tried several names but that fit and became his name. I found an improvement in the salt to be packed. This was all block salt, where I had only rock salt to pack before the war. I had made some frames to pack blocks with. They were made to hang on the pack saddle and hold two blocks on each side. The blocks were held in place by straps made of broken breast straps. I had never packed either of these horses before, but I got them loaded and went out on the forest. I came to an open park of good size and unloaded a block of salt off Shit-Head when he pulled away and proceeded to buck his load off.

I stood there holding Vinegar while this was happening. When that was done Vinegar pulled away from me and bucked his load off. There were all 8 blocks in one place. I gathered them up, reloaded with no further trouble, and started up higher. This was right at July 1st and the mosquitoes were around in

Me Packin' salt on Shit-Head as Vinegar looks on.

clouds. I was riding Silver, a small gray horse that had been on the outfit before I left for the war. I was going along when Silver switched at the mosquitoes and got the lead rope under his tail and proceeded to buck. I leaned way over trying to get the rope out when he spun towards me and I lit on the ground. Nobody saw that either, and then and there I tailed that rope on (tied it to Silver's tail). That worked fine until Shit-Head pulled back causing Vinegar to pull back, stripping the new pack saddle off Shit-Head. All three horses ended up in a pile, and lucky me, I never lost any hide in that wreck. I made it to the Shafer Ranch and stayed that night. There was more salt there to be packed out, which I finished with no more trouble. But that Shit-Head would always pull back if trees looked too close.

That was a busy summer for me, learning the country and how the cattle worked, branding the calves, getting the bulls scattered. All cow work but in a new location.

When fall came the Springsteads were moved to the Hill Ranch as the Hamiltons had taken a job in Wyoming. Johnny fed the hay and Frances learned to trap muskrats.

Mrs. Gus McDaniels was somewhat younger than Gus. She must have been farm raised, because in the spring of 1946 she got a lot of baby chicks and raised them. Towards fall she would dress a chicken or two for a small price. I recall stopping there when I was going to the Helena ditch and cow camp, where we had Lindsey Coe staying. He looked after the Pleasant Valley ditch during irrigation season. We would take him two or three horses and he would prowl around the forest looking after cattle. We planned on riding Stump Park and Davis Peak the next day. I stopped at McDaniels and got a fryer to take along for lunch the next day. I spent the night with Lindsey. The next morning he fried the chicken while I buttered some bread. We were to have a picnic. I wrapped the coffee thermos, the bread and butter in my slicker, and tied it on back of my saddle. We saddled up right by the porch, mounted up and were on our merry way. When it came lunch time, Lindsey had left his slicker on the porch, so we had bread and butter, and coffee for lunch. I stayed that night so I could partake of that fried chicken.

Lindsey was a good storyteller, and I liked the way he would tell me where he had been and what he had been doing. Example. "Yesterday me and Pete (who was a horse) were over in Onion Park, or Frog Draw." He always spoke of his horse as another person. We had cattle on Beaver and Line creeks, and when it came time to put the bulls out, Lindsey took 6 or 8 bulls and went from the Shafer Ranch past Big Creek Lake.

Lindsey told me of the time he met a dude woman who asked him, "Are you a cowboy"? He allowed he was, and she asked, "Where is your gun?" His reply was, "Hell lady, I'm past 60 years old and I don't need a gun."

Lindsey Coe about 1910.

The fishermen used to ask Lindsey where to find the best fishing. There was always a snowdrift you could see high up, and he would tell them, "See that snowdrift? Well, there is a stream on one side and a lake on the other side, and the fish go from that lake to the stream every morning and go back to the lake at night. The best way to get a lot of fish is to get them with a club as they cross that snowdrift!"

For a couple of winters Lindsey cooked in the cookhouse at the Hanson. I used to be in the kitchen and Lindsey would get to talking. If he ever had a hot pad I never saw such, but he had an old pair of jersey gloves that he kept on the warming oven. He would put them on to handle anything hot. He would get to talking and forget the gloves, burn his hand, then cuss and throw things.

Lindsey had been cow foreman for The Big Creek outfit many years before and told of many experiences. Big Creek trailed the cattle to Laramie to ship in the old days, and would hold them many miles out of Laramie while waiting for cattle cars. Lindsey being boss rode into town one time to see about cars, and stayed in and got somewhat drunk.

He was riding a green horse and as he was starting back, his horse suddenly grabbed himself and ran. Lindsey got him slowed down, rode a ways, and it happened again. Then after a while he got him slowed down again. Lindsey looked back, and found that a man on a bicycle had been catching up with him and scaring that bronc.

Lindsey told of when he used to bootleg and was delivering moonshine to a camp back in the woods. He took orders by phone. If they ordered, say, 10 sacks of oats and 3 bales of hay, he knew they wanted 10 pints and 3 gallons of moonshine. He told me of one time when he took hay, grain, and moonshine to a timber camp over towards Hog Park. Maybe on Damfino Creek he saw a blond headed girl who had 3 towheaded youngsters in a box on a hand sled. He watched her climb a hill among the trees; she was on skis. Lindsey said, "All at once here she came down among the trees. I thought she would batter the brains out of those little kids on those trees but she didn't. She just turned around and climbed the hill again for another run."

Lindsey was a gambler. One winter he got to gambling as a houseman in a Pan-Gee Game that went on continually in Walden. He would leave for town on Saturday and ask me to cook while he was gone. In winter I lived in the Hanson bunkhouse and wasn't always that busy, so I'd cook. He would come back Sunday evening, or sometimes he would show up on Monday, which got worse when he started going to town on Friday. I had to put a stop to it. I just told him enough was enough, and with that he quit. No hard feelings.

Lindsey Coe was born in Wyoming and brought to North Park as a 2-year old in 1882. He grew up here and went to

school in Walden where this yarn took place. Lindsey said that
he and several big boys were, should I say, unruly. They had
run off two women teachers, then a man teacher showed up.
Soon after school had taken up, he said they got to scuffling
and pretty soon they were jumping over the desks. That man
teacher got up, put on his hat, and walked out. They looked at
each other and said, "He sure didn't last long."

In due time the teacher returned. He had gone down town
and bought a riding quirt. He walked to the teachers desk,
slapped the desk with the quirt, and said, "You little bastards,
do you see this?"

Lindsey said, "Yes, and what are you going to do with it?"
Turns out he spoke when he should have been listening!

Here I had better catch up before going forward. I had been
having some health problems before I left the Army. After I
went to work for The Big Horn, I had more problems, so I
contacted The Veterans Administration. They had me go to the
Veterans Hospital in Cheyenne in July, 1946. I stayed a couple
of days, and they ran many tests. When the report came back it
said, I was "malnourished." Could be because I was under 130
pounds. In 1947 the Veterans Administration had me go to
Fitsimmons Hospital in Denver in February. They ran many
tests. As the weather warmed up I needed to get outdoors.
George Fleming, an army buddy of mine, was in the next ward.
He had been wounded in the hip by shrapnel. The fall before
they had healed up the wound and sent him home for hunting
season in Jackson Hole, Wyoming. He had continued to get
worse and came back to Fitsimmons where they opened his hip
and found they had left a piece of gauze inside the wound and
it had healed up over it! George was in a wheelchair and I pushed
him around outside for exercise. After I had spent over 4 weeks
there and nothing was happening, I hunted up the officer in
charge. I told him he could either discharge me or I would
AWOL! I got discharged and went back to work. One Vet
Hospital wanted to take out my appendix. The other suggested

they take out my gallbladder. Years later I went to Dr. France in Walden and he had x-rays taken. He called me in and announced, "*WE* have ulcers," and he was right.

In the spring of 1947 Waldo brought home an Indian named Joe. He wanted to break horses, and we ran in 15 head of those 5- and 6-year old half-thoroughbreds. Joe got them half broke, then got drunk and quit or got fired.

Many changes took place in 1947. McDaniels left the Boettcher Ranch and was replaced by the Wayne Geers, who were replaced on the Shafer Ranch by Si Dow. John McCasland left the Hunter Ranch and was replaced by Harry Oberg. The Gavins stayed at the Hanson until 1948. The Springsteads moved back to Lake Creek for the summer of 1947, them left to find a place of their own in Arkansas.

I had various help off and on. I had a fellow from the Sandhills of Nebraska calve the heifers on the Hanson Ranch in 1947. In the spring of 1948 I hired Duane Hagler. I was never a lone cow outfit again. Duane was from Nebraska. I always had help no matter what! He was always there at the end of the trail. When I came back from Fitsimmons in the spring of 1947 the VFW had bought a building and were going to open a club. That sounded good to me. No bunkhouse on The Big Horn had a shower because there was no running water in any of them. I like my drinks but never was a hand to set around bars, and this club sounded good. I joined the VFW Post and club. They had taken over the North Park Rodeo the year before, but had lost the rodeo grounds east of town. But there was a place to go. I think that Jackson County had already built a grandstand north of Walden, a lonesome grandstand east of the airport, with not a stick of fence in front of it. This was where the VFW was to build rodeo facilities. I laid it out one evening by car lights. I recalled the rodeo grounds in Greeley (where I had been bucked off). It took a lot of work to have it ready to have a rodeo in the middle of July. We needed corrals, pens, bucking chutes, catch pens, and a calf roping chute. I got that too close

to the bucking chutes and the calves would tend to turn away
from a right-handed roper. They were moved toward the race
track. That was the only alteration that had to be done from my
original blueprints. In 1947 the first rodeo was held in front of
the grandstand. Buck Yarborough furnished the stock except
for the bareback bucking horses. They were furnished by The
Big Horn. There were over 25 head just to have a few extra,
and we limited the entries to 25.

Those half-thoroughbreds that Joe the Indian broke were
the bulk of those bareback bucking horses, and the remainder
were hay horses that were handy.

One rodeo Duane and I had brought the bareback horses
from the Hanson Ranch and we came early, up the Hiway from
Cowdrey. Duane was riding a little buckskin that had come
from a wild bunch. Duane rode Buck on into town and in the
parade. When we went back up to the rodeo grounds, there
were several cars already there, and nobody had been selling
tickets, so everyone was trying to get caught up on selling tickets. Someone asked Duane to go to the gate and get some more
tickets. He rode in between two cars, handed the tickets to
someone, then had to back Buck out. In those days the bumpers
stuck out some, and Buck got a hock hooked and threw a fit.
We had planned on putting Buck in as a bareback horse.

I thought he was a little gimpy, but Duane said, "Go ahead
and put him in, and if he don't fire, give a re-ride." We slapped
a number on him and put him in the drawing. The guy that
drew him came out as mad as a wet hen. He had paid his entry
and here was a horse that had sweat under a saddle and was
still wet!

I told him, "If he don't buck hard enough to get you into the
money, I'll give you a horse that will." That rider lasted just
three jumps! In the three years we furnished the bareback horses
we never had a horse injured. By the way, the going contract
price for each bareback horse was $5.

Duane Hagler rassling calves at Wattenbergs about 1948.

While I was a member of the VFW Club they never put in a shower, but they did put in a Bottle Club whereby each drinker could keep his personal bottle. Soon I was listening to the same drunken chatter as in the bars. So I became an ex-member.

After three years as manager of the arena I gave up. I could never find out if the rodeo made money or lost money. But they did have wide open gambling during rodeo and the VFW got a percentage. The VFW also bought beer wholesale and sold it at the rodeo. I'm sorry, but I felt those two projects took precedence over the rodeo. They both made money!

Buck Yarborough bought those Indian Joe horses from Waldo, except for the only black horse, which The Big Horn kept. Buck kept a couple in his string and the rest were shipped to California.

We had this black horse at Lake Creek and put him in the barn where we had a bronc stall. We saddled him up and turned him out into the corral where he bucked the saddle. Duane watched, then said, "Hell, he can't buck. I'll ride him." He

named him Joe right there. Duane broke Joe. Joe stampeded
with Duane in the timber one time, but Duane stayed with him
and was the worse for wear. He was scratched, skinned, black
and blue, but was still there when Joe stopped!

We were taking dry cows to the Red Hill pasture from the
Lake Creek corrals. Things were moving slow when Joe came
undone and bucked Duane over the saddle horn the first jump.
Somehow Duane reached around behind and got ahold of the
saddle horn, went a jump or two and then said, "Hell I'll start
over." He turned loose and picked himself up and got back on
and Joe never offered to buck again that day. Duane rode Joe
for several years. He always said, "If Joe's back is dry, I am
never afoot." Joe stepped on a crooked limb in the forest and it
turned up and punctured him between the hind legs. Infection
set in and we lost Joe.

Duane had a way with all animals. One rodeo Duane armed
himself with a piece of pipe, got into the pen with the Brahma
bulls, and loaded them into the chute with very little commotion. The owner of the bulls admitted he had never seen them
handled as quietly. I have seen Duane take a plumb green horse
in the morning at Lake Creek, and work him in the round corral, ride him around the lake, then put 4 shoes on him all in the
same day.

Warren Stultz worked for us in the summer of 1948. He
was from eastern Colorado, and had his own horse and a dinky
trailer. He was attending Aggies in Ft. Collins. He and Duane
were fun and a lot of help in more ways than one.

After we opened the cow camp at Lake Creek in 1946, I
bought groceries at the Red and White Store in Walden. That is
where I met my future wife, Grace Case. She waited on me and
it got so nobody else would do.

I asked her for a date in the spring of 1948. I had bought a
car by then and we went to a dance at the Community Building
(the VFW Building now). As I drove into the parking lot I got

Warren Stultz, Duane Hagler, and Oley Kohlman by the bunk-house at Lake Creek in 1948.

stuck before we got to the front door. A kind soul with a pickup pulled us out.

Grace and her folks, her father Carlos, and mother Esther, ran a general merchandise store that sold everything from perfume to dynamite. That spring I ordered a keg (100 pounds) of size no. 1 horse shoes from Carlos. They cost 19¢ a pound.

I used to go to town Saturday evening. I'd go to the barber shop, shower and clean up, then go to the store. They stayed open on a Saturday evening because many ranch people came to town then. Grace's mother Esther brought supper for everyone on Saturday evenings, and I would be included.

Grace learned to be a butcher during the war, back when beef came in quarters. When the store closed I would help Grace clean up the butcher shop, before we could go to the late show. If Duane and Warren would get to town before me they would tell Grace that I wasn't able to come to town, and they were supposed to take her to the show! As I said, they were *lots* of help and *lots* of fun.

In the days after World War II there was a lot of volunteer work that went on. Reverend Walter Brunner was building the Community Church in Walden. Waldo sang in the choir and he got me to help several days on building that church. One time I went to an Easter program with the Gavins and son Mike. Probably Waldo sang.

Anyway toward the end Mike, who was about 3, wanted to go home. He was told, "Just one more song." We had one more, then there was to be another. About that time Mike said in a loud voice, "Let's go, we've had one more!"

Here is a little about the owner of The Big Horn, Clendennan Ryan. He was a grandson of Thomas Fortune Ryan, who was some sort of famous financier of bygone days, reputed to be among the wealthiest men. I got to know Clendennan well through the years. He was the first of his family to buy any western real estate. He had been in politics, and had been a sort of a stand-in for Mayor LaGuardia of New York City. He owned several dairy farms in New Jersey, and he dealt as well on Wall Street. He had been born rich and grew up rich. As I was around him we talked of many things. He spent one whole evening telling me about different ways people had tried to work him out of money. It was quite an education for me, who had never ever thought of having money in any amount. Mr. Ryan brought his son Mike out when he was five, also son Cyr was five when he too came out to the ranches. At first they opened the Old Lodge for a couple of summers and then Mr. Ryan decided to build a new lodge. I suggested the grove of trees on the old Lee Conrad homestead southwest of the Shafer Ranch.

I was told, "There are trees everywhere back East, we want to see out." The location was selected where Fort Boettcher now stands. I remember that the Fort was built in 1948, because it was in that year that Mr. Ryan wanted to take a pack trip, which we did. We left from the Old Lodge. There were Mr. Ryan and son Mike, Ryan's brother-in-law John Rutherford, and his twin sons Eric and Ian, who were under 10. It was decided that a trip to Steamboat Springs was what they wanted to do. Working for me at Lake Creek were Duane Hagler and Warren Stultz. Neither had packed a horse, but were good boys, and Waldo scared us up a cook. His name escapes me, but he had been haying for Si Dow on the Shafer Ranch. John Rutherford was a big man who stood over 6 foot 6. We had a hard time finding a saddle big or long enough in the stirrups, but we cobbled one up.

As we were packing up at the old Lodge I asked Duane and Stultz to take John and see if the saddle was going to be satisfactory. It was on a bay mare tied to a small quaker tree. Instead of untying her John climbed up on her and she pulled back. The tree started toward her and then she did pull back. Finally the halter rope broke and she went over backward with John. He had been a football player and had a trick shoulder that was thrown out of joint. He told us what to do. It amounted to me sitting on his head and Duane popping it back in. I guess the saddle fit because John made the trip with us all the way. There were nine of us plus five pack horses, so it took quite awhile to get packed and on our way.

There was not a smoker among us. After we got started I discovered that there was not a match along. I stopped at Ted Fliniaus', and the Missus gave me a box of matches. We went to Red Canyon and up that trail to the top. I do not recall where we nooned up but do recall John Rutherford claimed he had lost the cork out of a bottle of Scotch that he had tied on the back of his saddle. To save the Scotch we tried to drink it. We reached the top near sun down and went to North Lake to camp for the night. We had to hobble all the horses. They had some bells hung on them and were turned loose after dark. I listened for bells off and on all night. At first light I was up and discovered old Ike had not left, but there was not another bell to be heard. I started a fire, got the cook up and told him, "You get breakfast and get everybody up and fed, I do not know how long I may be gone." I rode off on Ike, followed the tracks and found the horses about two miles toward home. I caught and unhobbled them and returned to camp where most were up but the fire had gone out. Some cook!

We did get fed, packed up, and on our way. We spent a memorable day riding along the top, an all day trip without a cloud in the sky. This was near the middle of September. We arrived at Summit Lake, and before we unpacked I made a hurry-up trip to my old cow camp. I found a couple of Forest Service men camped there, so we unloaded and made camp at the lake.

I had planned a menu for each meal and thought we had enough food, but that last morning we were out of bread. I had Bisquick, so I made biscuits in a dutch oven.

I was out of practice and didn't wait for good enough coals, and the biscuits were too dark on the bottom and too blond on top. The Ryan bunch thought they were great anyway.

I had called the dude ranch in Strawberry Park before we left home and made reservations with the Bob Swineharts who ran it. I knew them from my days on top in the 30's.

I suggested we go to Longs Lake and down the Fish Creek canyon. The Ryans wanted to go direct, so we packed up and went down the Buffalo Pass road and got to Strawberry Park before noon. I had not ordered lunch, but Mrs. Swinehart got us lunch and Ryans wanted to get home immediately! They did some telephoning, and got an old pickup to come and haul them back to The Lodge.

Here I might explain what was on that load. There were 7 people, 3 kids, and 4 men. There were 7 saddles, 7 bed rolls, 4 pack saddles and panniers and whatever duffel that they may have had along.

The pickup was loaded to near the top of the cab, so the 4 men sat on top of that, and the 3 kids were able to squeeze in with the driver. They got away by late afternoon, and went over Rabbit Ears Pass. They got to Colorado Creek, and the bridge was torn out. It was being rebuilt, and they had to go back and go through Clover Valley, past Johnsons and did not get home until 10 o'clock that night. This was in September and the nights got cold. Those men on top of the load were nearly frozen.

Duane Hagler and I stayed to bring the horses back the next day. We kept one bedroll and one packsaddle.

Before they left Mr. Ryan told me to have a bill sent. I said no, I had better settle while I am here. We had to take the horses to another ranch for the night. There was a meal for 9 people of which only 2 were eaten, and there was the lunch for 9 that we had not ordered. I had my checkbook along and settled before we left the next morning.

Clendennan Ryan was reputed to be among the country's most wealthy men, but he never seemed to have any money on him. Waldo met him and his two sons in Laramie one trip and he bought the boys each a straw hat. It came to 6 or 8 dollars, and he had to borrow the money from Waldo.

Duane and I took our time, came back over Buffalo Pass and made it to Albert Manvilles that evening. The next morning we puttered and only made it to Wattenbergs for lunch as we were going back to batch at Lake Creek. Ryans left for Denver and the East the next day. Warren Stultz was going to Aggies in Fort Collins and left as soon as they got back, and Waldo paid the cook off. We stopped at Wattenbergs before noon and Elmer was in Walden, so Eva had us come in and wait.

When Elmer got home he told us of a burglary in Walden the night before. A couple of guys had gone through the Chedsey Hotel where there were several drunk hay hands. They stole any money that was to be had, then stole a car on main street, and headed north out of town. Someone saw them take the car and followed them as far as the restaurant on the hill north and caught them there. When we found out who they were it turned out to be our trip cook and his brother. They had been out on parole, and were now back in jail.

Mr. Ryan spent some time every summer at the Old Big Horn Lodge, and later at Fort Boettcher. At first he brought son Mike then Cyr. John Rutherford and his twins were out at least 2 summers. Of the 4 boys Cyr was my favorite. I took the boy riding many times. Mike always wanted to ride "full speed." The horses that they rode were not full speed horses. All had some age on them but where it was level and no holes we did ride "Full Speed."

One summer I was coming to Walden and the Ryan boys came with me. When we got to town I asked what they wanted to do, and they said, "We want to see a jail!" Bert Geer was custodian at the court house, so we went and they saw the jail inside and outside.

One summer the Ryans and the Rutherfords were staying at the Old Lodge and wanted to go camping. There was a man cook there so was decided we would pack up to Peggy or Blue Lake, and spend a night. We took a couple of pack horses and got up there well before supper time, got the camp set up, and some of us went fishing. I was fishing at the inlet when a little shower came up while the sun was still shining. The fish started to hit, I had 2 flies on and would wait until there was a fish on each fly. Those trout were 15 or 16 inches long. It was the best fly fishing I ever had. The cook fried fish for supper. Mike Ryan was 7 years old, and he ate 7 fish for supper. Neither he or his dad got much sleep that night.

The two years after Fort Boettcher was built, there was much more company from the east. There was Mr. Ryan's doctor from New York City, a Dr. Fleming and wife Zia.

Zia had been a Zigfield Follies girl before she married the doctor. She was a very delightful person to know. We had poker games many evenings at Ft. Boettcher. Doc was rather bossy as far as Zia went, and he would tell her how to play the game. Invariably she would listen, then say "I am sorry" and rake the pot in. Zia gave me a pocket knife that I still have after these many years.

I told Dr. Fleming about having dropsy in cattle. He recommended that I try a diuretic that came for humans. Later I tried it. It helped, but was no cure.

Speaking of medicine I was probably the first to give penicillin to an animal in North Park. We had some young Hereford bulls and one of the best got pneumonia and was wheezing. I went to Walden and got penicillin. It came in small vials, probably 1cc each. I drained many and gave it to the bull for a couple of days and he recovered.

Dr. Keithly was a veterinarian who was also county extension agent. He taught me many things, like the proper way to stitch up a prolapse cow, and how to float a horse's teeth. In the summer of 1948 we had the flats gathered and around 1,100 pairs in the Lake Creek field when we began to find dead cattle. We never lost any calves. It was mostly cows. One evening I went north and saw a bull grazing right by the gate into the Hill Ranch. The next morning as I rode that same way there was that bull dead.

The bull had no sign of being sick, and there he was dead. I called Dr. Keithly. He came out and we went over that area, but could not find any poison of any kind. Doc insisted it had to be poison. Finally I said, "I'm going to post this bugger." I opened him up and Doc came over and asked me if I could locate the spleen. I did and it looked like a clot of blood. Doc said, "I have never seen anthrax, but this looks suspicious." We took specimens and sent them to the lab at Aggies in Fort Collins. It was diagnosed sure enough as anthrax. The first thing Dr. Keithly asked was, "Do you have skin broken on your hands?" I did. I had a rope burn on one finger. I do not recall if we consulted a medical doctor or not. I was to have 3 shots of penicillin a day, 8 hours apart! Waldo volunteered to administer same. I went down to the Hanson Ranch every night to get my night shots in the fanny for nearly a week.

Believe me, I stood tall in the saddle as we gathered those 1,100 cows, and vaccinated them in two days! Whatever we gave them, it worked and they quit dying. The loss was around 20 head of cows and that 1 bull.

Each spring after that we vaccinated all the cows for anthrax up close to calving time. That gave Duane and I something to do, getting the snow and ice out of 4 chutes and alleys and getting the gates working. We found that coal slack scattered around helped, and iced-in gates called for half-sticks of dynamite.

In 1950 again we were losing cows in the Lake Creek field. Dr. Keithly had left, and Dr. Jim Pitcher had replaced him. I called him and he and his wife Arlete came. They were sort of newlyweds. As we posted a fresh dead cow, Doc called out big words and Arlete wrote them down. I was impressed. I had been around cows all my life but had never heard those words before.

That epidemic turned out to be Malignant Edema, so again we vaccinated those 1,100 cows and it stopped. The loss was less than half this time. Malignant Edema vaccine was included with Black-Leg vaccine in those days. We started vaccinating the replacement heifers twice.

The worst job I had was doctoring diphtheria in those 300 replacement heifers on the feed ground in winter. Diphtheria ran through them every winter. It would start about January and last for a month or so. The calves would get sores in the mouth and on the tongue. To doctor you would catch the calf, throw it, and pull out the wad of hay that the calf could not swallow. I carried a steel spoon some 10 or 12 inches long that I cleaned the sore out with. Generally there would be several sores to doctor. After the sores were scraped clean I would take cotton in a pair of forceps to make a swab. I would dip this in carbolic acid and swab out the sores. Carbolic acid froze easily, and had to carried in an inside pocket.

I spent many an afternoon doctoring diphtheria calves. The last couple of years we took to feeding those infected calves alfalfa cubes or pellets. They could soak them up and swallow them.

We raised colts every year. Besides that half-Thorough-bred, half-Morgan stud that I used for a winter horse, Waldo bought a Tennessee Walking stud and a Quarter Horse stud. Along in the 40's they were beginning to register Quarter Horses. If you wanted to register a quarter horse they would send a man around to evaluate him. Whoever evaluated that stud didn't pass him. A lot depended on who you were, we decided.

In the first crop of colts out of the half and half stud, there were 8 stud colts that I halter broke, and rode them all bareback in the big barn on the Hanson Ranch. Waldo gave me two of those colts. There was one colt I didn't want. I named him Monty, and he was ill natured. He kicked me once while I was feeding him oats. Later he turned out to be an outlaw.

Waldo bought another Belgian stud, not related to the old stud. He was a three year old that Duane and I decided to work with. We hitched him with another horse. It was winter so we hitched to a sled. We drove around some then we decided to cross the Platte on the ice. The ice was slick, and the new stud slipped, got down, and could not get up. We had to get another team and pull him off the ice. We never hitched him up again.

When I first came back those two year old colts were so full of botts they would nearly die in the spring. Then phe-nothiazine came on the market in powder form only. There were no boluses then. We got capsules and filled them with phe-nothiazine, and gave them with a balling gun. We treated all the horses on The Big Horn, over 300 head broke and unbro-ken. We fixed up a chute at the Hill Ranch where we could treat the unbroken ones. After that the horses wintered better.

There were always lousy cows and bulls. They could be treated with whatever we had, generally some form of dip. The next year they would be greasy with lice again. There never was a sure cure for lice until Warbex and Rulene came along.

Those two eliminated heel flies which used to hit a bunch of cattle and scatter them. Many would find a tall clump of sage-brush, and lie down in it out of sight.

Many's the time heel flies took a bunch of cattle away from us on the Flats. Sometimes we would get part of them regath-ered, and sometimes we would have to give up and come back another day.

Woody Tongue was a common occurrence in cattle. We used potassium iodine in crystal form. It would be administered by capsule for 2 or 3 days in a row, until the cow's skin began to look like rusty flakes next to the hair.

Lumps were mostly cut open to drain, sometimes we would inject some Titchner of Iodine. There was a Dr. Sailer, a short fat man but a darn good veterinarian. He treated lumps with a white powder that was put on cotton gauze and inserted into the lump and a stitch taken to hold it in. Eventually the inside of the lump would come out, cotton and all, and the lump would heal rather smooth. Waldo finally learned what that powder was. I have forgotten.

Around the start of the 1950's, sulfas began to show up. They were the first boluses that I recall.

All calves had horns, and we never did anything about them until fall. Then they were dehorned with a dehorning saw. We had chutes at all locations. They were 2 man chutes and the squeeze was the far side. It was hinged at the bottom, with weights hung on a rope that ran over a pulley to pull it back open. A rope from the squeeze passed over a pulley on top of a post, a pole that worked on a bolt at the bottom that the rope was tied to. A man raised the pole to open the chute and pulled down on it to squeeze the calf.

To hold the head secure for the operation, a wagon wheel was hung between two posts so it would turn. There were two pulleys. One was placed so a rope fastened solid to the right of the calf's head and then ran thru a pulley to hold the nose still. Then the rope went thru another pulley that pulled the head down. There was a squeeze man and a head man necessary to operate those chutes.

There were two main weanings, one at the Boettcher Ranch and the other at the Hill Ranch. Generally there would be 1,000 to 1,100 head at the Boettcher, including the Shafer cows. At the Hill Ranch there would be 300 to 350 pair to be weaned another day.

The Boettcher weaning was the big one. We gathered the cows toward evening, put them in the lot south of the corrals. It was all buck fence. Weaning day we would separate the calves from the cows. We had an alley with a section of the poles on one side that we let down. They were low enough for a calf to go under and high enough to keep the cows in the alley. Of course we sifted calves out as we let the cows out. We always worked off 50 or so cows that we were going to ship to drive with the calves. When all was ready Duane, Waldo, and I would turn the calves out east and head for The Gap. We each would have a tin can with some rocks in it to shake to put the go into that many calves going away from their mothers. As soon as we dropped thru The Gap, they could no longer see or hear their mothers. Generally the cows we had along would make a good lead and the calves strung fairly well.

Only once did we have a goof-up! We had a ranch hand who wanted to help, so we put him on a horse and gave him a can of rocks. He pushed the calves too hard and they could not all get through the gate by the old Club House, so they split, some going south and some going north. We had just brought the pairs from the Shafer Ranch the afternoon before. A splinter of calves headed north and they got a goodly way to the bridge. It was some 2 or 3 miles before we got them turned around and back to the bunch that had gone back to where the cows were in the lot. It was noon before we got away from the Boettcher and it was dark when we hit a lane some 2 miles west of the Hanson Ranch. When we got to the Platte Bridge we met a car but managed to get it through and not get turned around. The next day Duane and I went back with the pickup and were able to haul all the calves that we had wasted in the pickup in one load. Those were long days, but it worked if you did it right.

One trip, Waldo, Duane, and I went to the Boettcher Ranch to get ready to wean. It was blowing and snowing so hard we ate lunch there and drove to the Hill Ranch and decided to wean that bunch. George Rose was contracting there. We sorted off our cull cows and the calves. There were some 300 head. We got George to take some hay on a sled and lead us as far as Dead Horse hill, then he turned back. We got across Placer Draw on top to go into Ruby Gulch. There was a snowdrift there, and the lead cows had gone through and were out of sight. Those calves balked! We three spent until nearly dark and only lost about 200 yards before they gave up and we came on to the Hanson Ranch with no further trouble. We had no tin cans of rocks that trip.

The bulk of the steer calves were sold and delivered soon after weaning. We sorted off 300 replacement heifers and took the rest to the Great Western Sugar Factory in Loveland, Colorado. The Big Horn had an agreement with the sugar company where we used their feed lots at the factory. The cull cows and cows that had hairball calves were fed wet pulp and some alfalfa hay to winter. The calves were sent along with the cows and turned out to be respectable calves by spring. There was a man who lived in Loveland who took care of that operation. It was a winter job. When we had any dropsy cattle that was where we took them.

We were beginning to ship by truck, but many's a railroad car we loaded. We always said, "There we won't have to turn those again."

Branding was done as we gathered the flats. We would gather a bunch and brand the calves in a corral at the southeast corner of the Hill Ranch meadow. Where the Hill, the Lake Creek and the open range met, there was one big square corral.

It was nothing fancy. There were no gates as long as I was around, but there were poles that we slid in between posts for gates on each end.

We also used the dipping corrals at Lake Creek for branding. Many times we would gather from the close flats and brand them there. Those Big Horn cows and calves were not easy to corral. This is the way we did it. We would take them past the corral where we had a wing to throw them against and back them in. As we got the close ones gathered, we would gather smaller bunches and brand them coming in at the square corral. When Duane and Warren were there we used to guess how many calves there were going to be and bet. Those monkeys would get me to write down my guess, then they would put one number higher, and one number smaller than mine. One day we were drifting a bunch in that I managed to get a count on. Unknown to them I won that one.

One spring Duane was over at the Boettcher. I got a bright idea and asked him to shut the gates from Lake Creek to the open range when there were about 200 calves in and we would brand that many before they went out. Duane called and Waldo and I took 2 ranch hands to rassle and went over. Duane had them partly bunched and when we tried to corral them I knew we were in trouble. They would not all go into the corral, and we had to let some out on the north end. Then when we had them in the south end we backed those in and it held them. Then it showered, but by noon we were able to brand, and brand we did until after 6 o'clock, some 400 calves. Duane roped, Waldo branded, and I castrated, ear marked, and vaccinated. Those two rasslers got so tired that they would grab a calf without getting up. The calves were small enough that it worked. Duane generally roped and I generally cut, ear marked, and vaccinated. The vaccine came in 10, 50, or 100 doses per bottle. As the branding progressed I'd ask Duane, "How many more?" The answer was always the same, "Pretty many," so I never knew which size bottle to open. Another habit I had was saving one earmark from each calf (we under bit both ears), then when we were done I would count the ear bits to get a count on calves done. In those days there seemed to be only one strain of black-leg. Now they have 7-way Blackleg combined with Malignant Edema. It was the only vaccine given at branding time. The replacement heifers were always vaccinated in the fall for Bangs or Brucellosis but that had been started before I left for the war.

The winter of 1948-49 was one I recall. How well I remember the day before Christmas. Duane and I had gathered all surplus horses around the Hanson Ranch. We left with them after lunch and took a good 200 head across the Flats to the Boettcher Ranch on their way to the Shafer Ranch for the winter. I had a date so I returned across the Flats toward sundown. There was a good 2 feet of snow, it covered all sage brush, but that many horses had knocked the snow out of a strip 20 or 30 feet wide. As I rode back, there were literally thousands of sage chickens feeding along our trail. I never saw as many sage chickens any time after that winter.

There was a bunch of cows being fed at the Boettcher Ranch southwest of Fort Boettcher. Duane and I were by there after the first of the year and the snow was stirrup deep. The wind came up several days later and blew the snow away. There was a lot of bare stubble showing after that blow. The cows had taken shelter behind some willows but the willows blew full of snow and there was only the tops showing. When that happened, the cows drifted and some of them got into a drain ditch. We lost 3 or 4 cows. Those surviving cows were a sight! The hair had been scoured off their hocks and pin bones by the wind blowing the snow.

The hay there had been put up real late and did not have much feed value. Wattenbergs, whose upper place was south of there, had some hay they would sell. Waldo and I joined Harry and Elmer Wattenberg to measure those stacks. We ended up poking a shovel handle down through the snow, and measuring the shovel handle to get an estimate of the stack measurement.

Part of the horse drive going into Lake Creek from The Gap.

So those three or four cows were the only livestock loss that The Big Horn had in the famous winter of 1949.

Come February 18th it was still cold but the wind had quit. Duane and I took a team and sled from the Hanson Ranch, went to Cowdrey where the Jeep was, and drove to Walden. We had grocery lists for at least four households on The Big Horn. That was Duane's 21st birthday and I took him into a bar and bought him a drink! That day marked the end of problem weather for 1949. Sure we had weather, but not *THAT* kind of weather.

The winter of '49 was hard on the railroad into North Park because they got snowed in many times. By then we had mail service by stage as well as by rail.

We had a car load (25 head) of dry cows that we were trying to ship to the Denver market by rail. We took them to the Cowdrey stockyards three times but the train never got there so we would take them back to the Hanson.

Old Vic Hanson was brand inspector then. He had looked at them twice when we took them and put them in the stockyards for the third time. We rode over to the Cowdrey store and

One cold winter!

met Vic there. He asked if these were the same cows. Smart ass me said, "Sure they are the same cows but we only put 2 'V dots' in." (Ⅴ was the inspector's brand.) He borrowed my horse and went and looked. We finally got a truck to meet us at Peggy Hunter's, and got them on their way before the county roads were open. I took a team and sled with some hay to lead the cows through Cowdrey. South of Schilling's house or shop there was a snowdrift 10 or 12 feet high which was very steep on the east side. I worried about team, sled, and me ending up in a pile at the bottom, but the team jumped as they took off and we made it fine.

The summer of '49 we had a family from Missouri help us on Lake Creek named the Kimseys. Jewel, the Missus, cooked and Ed irrigated and built fence. Jimmy was about 12, and he sat on the corral fence and would watch us ride off. He would be sitting on the fence when we came back in sight that evening. We scraped up a saddle and asked if he wanted to ride with us. He did, and by fall he was a lot of help. One morning I told him to ride a horse that was hard to catch. Jimmy walked into the barn and got a rope and snared that old pony the first loop. We surmised he had done some practicing, and had got down off that fence while we were out of sight. He also took care of our bum herd. We always had a milk cow at Lake Creek, always had her calf on her. When we were going to be gone we would leave the cow and calf together. When we wanted milk we would lock the calf up for a night and milk half, then turn the calf out for his share. Duane and I began collecting nurse cows. When we would see a likely cow, and find out if she was mild mannered we would bring her in. When we found a bum calf we would bring it in and put it on with another calf. In fact it got so that there was a calf for every tit on the place. We had a calf pasture and only let the cows in at night and morning. We had oats to feed and help what little milk they got. I'm not sure how many cows we had, but there were 25 respectable calves to add to the big bunch that fall. We weaned just over 1,800 calves which was a high for the 5 years I was there.

Bum calves showed up a lot of places. One time we were moving a bunch over Independence Mountain and ran across a bum calf with the bunch in Placer Draw. I took a piggin' string and tied it to a sage bush well off the road. When we got back to camp toward evening we got into a car and drove up through the Hill Ranch to pick up the bum. It was loose, someone must have seen it from the road and thought it was going to starve tied up. Here we were afoot, at sundown 5 or 6 miles from a horse. We caught that calf the hard way, we ran it down. Both of us were near wind-broke before we caught it. Some help don't help! Bum calves became bums when they were separated from their mothers or the mother died. First, let me say, all cows are not ideal mothers! Some care, some don't. Those Hereford cows had problems with sun burned bags (white bags are bad burners). A calf that has to depend on a burned bag for a living doesn't always succeed. First calf heifers have more trouble keeping track of their calves, but bumming among heifers was better than among cows, who kick visitors off. In heifers you could see a bum calf sneak up and steal a meal between the hind legs while the other calf sucked. Some bums made it while others did not. I always hated to see a bum calf that I couldn't help.

Helena, Colorado came to an end. There was a Swede bachelor named Pete who lived in Pearl year round. I do not recall what else he did but he trapped martin on Red Elephant Mountain in winter. Pete had a cabin in Helena, the last of the old town. The Big Horn had a newer cabin near there that Lindsey Coe stayed in summers. Pete used to snowshoe from Pearl to Helena, stay all night, run his traps on Red Elephant Mountain, make Helena for another night, and then head back to Pearl. One fall Pete asked me, "Do you ever ride that Helena country after there is snow on?"

I said, "Sure, I ride it every fall after we get plenty of snow looking for tracks."

He said, "Would you do me a favor?"

I said, "Sure." He asked if I would go into that cabin where I would find a coal-oil lamp, and would I pour the coal-oil around and set it afire? Then he explained that he was not going to trap anymore and that the fishermen made such a pig pen of his cabin every summer he thought that would be the best way to handle it. He felt the Forest Service would make a big production of it if he asked them! So when there was enough snow I rode that country for tracks, stopped in and burned the last of Helena.

Afterwards when Pete did not trap he moved down to Carl Carlstrom's and lived in a cabin there winters. I used to go there in the evenings and play cribbage with him. Some evenings Carl would be there playing cards with Pete, and they would take turns playing cribbage with me. We never had heard of a three handed cribbage board then.

After we were married I was telling Grace about burning that cabin, and she wanted to know what became of the lamp. I said, "It burned up! Wouldn't I have looked funny riding old Ike out through the snow belly deep carrying a lamp?"

There was another snow trip I made in that neighborhood late one fall. Foreman White called and wanted to know if I could go up to their cabin on the east shore of Big Creek Lake and drain it. I took old Ike again, and the snow was belly deep when we got there. Foreman told me there was some beer there. I found it and opened a bottle. It had almost frozen, and as I opened it, it gushed up, then turned to ice. I never bothered to pack any of that beer out but there were some spirits that didn't freeze to take the place of frozen beer. I do recall that Foreman presented me with a Pendelton Wool shirt for my trouble. Those were the days before snow machines, and when it snowed up, it was snowed up!

In that same neck of the woods, sometimes as we rode towards home around the east side of Big Creek Lake, there was only a trail there then, lots of moraines with up and down terrain. There was a big rock out in the lake that fishermen used to wade out and stand on to fish. Duane would creep up behind that little hill and flip a pebble out behind the fisherman, who would think a fish had taken a fly and it was fun to see the frenzy that the water was whipped into. After a decent lapse of time Duane would do it all over with the same results. Honest, we did do a hell of a lot of work besides the fun we had.

Mr. Ryan decided to sell The Big Horn. The new owners were a group of Texans headed by W.L. Vogler, and the deal was made in the spring of 1950. I helped inventory the livestock. I am at a loss as to the number of cattle, but I do recall there were 365 horses, one for every day of the year! Duane and I rode for the new outfit until the gathering was done, then we quit together, on November 1st, 1950. Duane went to the army and I returned to the Johnson place, thus ending my cowboy career that had covered some 12 years. I have never regretted the experience.

Lindsey Coe had a cousin Mamie Leek, who later married Billy Hill, an old time North Park cowboy. Mamie was the first girl in here to ride astride, with a man's saddle. "Proper" women rode side saddle back then. She also broke many a horse to ride, and was an "extra" in Hollywood. If I asked a question when we would get to talking about old times Mamie would say "Why ask me? I didn't come to North Park until 1895!"

I would like to share with you a poem that Mamie read at the 7th annual reunion of North Park Pioneers.

Early Day Cowboy Life In North Park
By Billy and Mamie Hill

Dear friends and old timers, if you'll lend me
   your ears
I'll tell you a tale of my cowpunching years.
In early days North Park could boast
Of Some big cow outfits and one of the most
Popular owners of cattle and land
Was Montie Blevins, and any cow hand
that was lucky enough to make his home
At the Moore and Blevins, never cared to
   roam.
The home ranch was located down Cowdrey
   way,
Where Mr. Hugh Hunter lives at the present
   day.
A wonderful cowman was Montie, he knew
   his stuff, —
A man we'll remember, for he did enough
To build North Park into choice stock land,
That the memory of him will ever stand.
In 1897, along the month of May,
Mr. Blevins started out and went up north-
   west way,
In a very short time he sent back word,
That up in Oregon he'd bought a herd
Of twelve hundred cows and was shipping
   them down,
To be met by his punchers in a Wyoming
   town.
Harry Green was foreman then;
And a good one too, for he knew his men,
And he knew a lot about a cow—
Believe it or not, he's a sheepman now.
Harry hired some good cowpokes,

We thought they were good, you may think
   they're jokes
There was Bill Brennan for cook, and a good
   cook too;
Bill sure stirred up a swell mulligan stew .
There was Wash Alderdice, you all know the
   lad,
We called him Josh from the habit he had,
Of joshing the world and everyone.
When Josh was along there always was fun.
Charlie Mitchell was "Mitch", or some called
   him "Ott".
He'd worked for Ott, the printer, so that name
   he'd got.
Clyde Webb we called Rusty from the red
   head he had.
And a rough ridin' waddy was that old Rusty
   lad.
There was Clarence Webb too, as good as
   you'd find.
The horse that he rode just as well made
   up his mind
To tend to his biz' and go right down the trail,
'Cause buckin' and bawlin' was sure to no
   avail.
Another good puncher was Fred McAvoy,
When you wanted things quiet, Fred sure
   was a joy.
Al Green was along and that kept things
   sunny;
His keen Irish wit made the whole world look
   funny.
And last of the list is myself, Billy Hill,

The others always to say Sorghum Bill,
'Cause if anything happened that at every
meal
I didn't get some kind of syrup, I sure made
a squeal.
Harry Green was called Monk and I never
knew why,
I've heard some folks say—but I think it's a
lie—
That when a small boy he'd herd monkeys
for days,
So he'd be a good foreman and know cow-
punchers ways.
We were all set and ready to be out on our
way,
When Harry got word from Montie one day
To be in Rawlins, Wyoming on the eighth of
June,
And none of us thought it a bit too soon.
Do you know the joy of cowpunching days,
When you hit the saddle in the mellow
haze
Of a cool spring morning in early June?
Then you know how we felt and we thought
that soon
With our bunch of cows we'd be coming
back
From this journey out to the railroad track.
So we started out with spirits gay,
And camped on Cow Creek at the end of
the day.
With supper over we helped with the dishes,
Then the cook expressed as one of his
wishes
A game of craps, and tho the game might
be brief,
We all of us said we'd just as lief.
So we smoothed out the trap on one of the
beds,
And all gathered 'round with nought in our
heads
But to get all the coin from the other six.
"Seven come eleven, now a Jimmy Hicks,
Phoebe on the mountain, Ada from Decada,
bones,
Come on Little Joe", and then some cuss'n'
groans.
At ten o'clock the game broke up, with
nothin' to keep it alive,
Al Green had all the cash in camp, three
dollars, seventy five,

So we crawled into our beds rolled out on
the ground,
Glad we didn't have to pack all that silver
around.
It was nice and warm with soft clouds floatin'
by,
And we all went to sleep out under the sky.
But next morning when we raised our heads,
Six inches of snow covered all our beds.
Mitchell and I, who were bedfellows then,
Just covered our heads right up again,
'Till the cook called "hot-stuff" out loud and
clear,
And we heard other punchers a-creepin'
near;
Then they jerked off the covers in a way
nothin' slow,
And dragged us around by the heels in the
snow.
Did you ever stamp into tight boots with high
heels
On a snowy morning? Then you all know
how it feels.
We stopped near Saratoga at eleven o'clock
that day.
And with snowed-on beds out dryin', the
world looked gay.
Then the boys all turned a longing eye out
toward the town,
And 'fore I knew it, I was left alone to hold
the old camp down.
I noticed as they rode away, they each one
seemed to strive
For a place 'long side of Banker Al and his
three dollars, seventy-five.
In about an hour one puncher rode in,
And his singin' and cryin' raised an awful
din.
Just what brand he'd been drinkin' was hard
to say,
Neither a cry nor a laugh jag but sort of two-
way.
Then he got the idea that he'd tear up the
camp—
And I knew on that notion I must put a
clamp—
So I lit in to catch him, and without much
bad luck,
Roped him and tied him to a big fence buck.
He was mad and seemed to blame me, if
you please.

I'll not tell what he called me 'cause I can't
speak Chinese.
Well, I cooked up some dinner, It was then
past noon,
And I figured the others would come along
pretty soon.
They all rode in later, some of 'em three
sheet in the wind,
But nothin' to speak of, as they just stood
and grinned.
When they saw what I'd tied up. He was
sleeping quite sound.
They'd been back sooner, they said, if they'd
known he was found.
After dinner we loaded up, rarin' to step.
But the more we shook that cowboy the
sounder he slept.
His horse was all saddled, but he couldn't
ride there,
And to leave him there sleepin', that wouldn't
be fair,
So we throwed him up high on the bedrolls
and tent,
Tied him down tight with ropes and onward
we went.
We got as far as Little Sage Creek that night,
And the next morning our waddy was feelin'
all right.
That day the road to Rawlins seemed a long
way around;
So we cut straight across where just cow
trails were found.
We were joggin' along in a half asleep way,
When all of a sudden we heard Rusty say,
"Hey boys! There's a rattler! Now just watch
him die"
And he was down off his horse in the wink
of an eye.
He wanted the rattles to take home to
show—
Some guys in North Park had never seen
'em you know.
The rattler started down a hole right by the
trail,
And it was almost out of sight when Rusty
grabbed its tail!
We stood there aghast at that boy's sand,
When the snake's head popped out again
right up by Rusty's hand!
It didn't take long for Clyde to make up his
mind,

That those weren't the rattles he was tryin'
to find.
He turned that snake loose with no more
delay,
He got on his horse and we all rode away.
We didn't say much but we felt kinda sick.
Who'd a thought a darn rattle snake could
double back so quick?
When we unloaded to get the grub, that
noon someone with a helping hand
Untied a rope that held things on and threw
it in the sand.
When dinner was ready the boys all gath-
ered 'round.
Filled cups and plates at the campfire and
sat on the ground.
With a cup of coffee in one hand, a plate of
biscuits and beans in the other,
Harry sat down cross-legged, cowboy style,
on the sand in front of his brother.
Al saw his chance in a second—for a better
chance he would never hope.
Poor Harry never knew 'till later that he was
settin' on the end of that rope.
We were scared to death of rattlers. Clyde's
stunt made us feel none too good.
We'd walk carefully 'round every sage brush,
stay in the open if we could.
Well, Al picked up the rope and pulled it with
a motion steady and sly,
Say! Harry, beans, biscuits, & coffee all shot
straight up toward the sky.
I've read some place that it's healthy to laugh
while eating your lunch,
If that's true, I'm right here to tell you that
day we was a darned healthy bunch.
We were in Rawlins that evening when the
sun went down,
Pitched camp by the stockyards and went
into town.
Harry got a telegram from Montie that night,
Saying a shipment would be there in a few
days, all right.
That was fine, we'd play around town for a
while;
So we all started out with a big broad smile,
But we soon found out that it wasn't no joke
To be tied up in town and every one of us
broke.
Even Harry, I don't think he'd have helped if
he could,

Guess he thought if we were broke it's a
cinch we'd be good.
Then one day he surprised us by handin'
each of us a five,
Said he'd met a man that owed him, did our
crowd come alive!
But we were all broke again in another day
or two,
And we lay around camp feelin' pretty darn
blue.
One evening five of us were strolling
about
With Wash among us, when he sings out,
"Boys, I've got money, and to show my
heart's right
I'll split it five ways and make the world look
bright.
Now, it's all in one chuck, you wait here," he
said
"And if I can get it busted, we'll paint the old
town red."
Gee, that sounded good, but our hearts kind
of sank,
'Cause all we could figure, was Josh had
robbed a bank.
He turned 'round and left us, went into a
cigar store,
It seemed like an hour before he came out
the door.
Then he walked up to us and with a swag-
ger grand,
And laid a little ol' nickel in each outstretched
hand.
"Now boys, you needn't worry 'bout payin'
this back right away,
Just when you get home and feelin' flush, I
know I'll get it some day,
Were up in the saddle and out on our way.
We trailed the cows about twelve miles out,
Where some springs in the hills were scattered about.
And there we held them 'till we'd get some
more of the twelve hundred cows we'd
come out there for.
They came in shipments of two hundred,
about, and every few days another shipment came out.
They drank so much water, we got scared
of a drought,
So we split up the bunch and took part of
them South

Three miles to some ore springs out under
the heavens,
And part went northwest where a rancher
named Nevins,
Had several reservoirs, not very large,
Where we could water the cows for just a
small charge.
Every morning in couples, we'd pocket a
lunch and start for a water hole with part
of the bunch.
As he built us a sandwich, Bill 'ud say with
a smile,
"I'm sure glad to be rid of you guys for a
while."
We grazed the cows to water every day;
And grazed them back a different way.
And all day long the grazed around;
And at night we worked 'em back again to
the same bed ground.
They weren't hard to guard after the first few
nights,
But some, now and then, seemed to think it
their rights
To start back home, up Oregon way.
So we had to stick around to persuade 'em
to stay.
Did you ever night herd till you got so darned
tired
You could stand up and sleep and you
hoped you'd get fired?
That's the way we all felt, when one night
Harry said
"Boys, I'll guard a little while, you can all go
to bed."
Well, we didn't stop to argue nor ask if it
was right
When we woke up from a good night's sleep,
Harry'd guarded alone all night.
Those are the things you won't forgit
When it's so hot and dusty you just can't
spit,
Or when a blizzard's on and it's forty below,
And your pet horse wallerin' to his belly in
the snow,
Or when things go so haywire you just want
to sob,
And you cuss cowpunchin' as the world's
worst job.
Then you think of the chap that hired you,
How he works right 'long side to help you
thru,

Just one of us fellers, never a bit high hat,
Say, you'd ride thru Hell for a boss like that.
The weather was so hot 'twas hard to keep
fresh meat,
And a rabbit or a sage chicken was sure a
dainty treat.
We'd bring them in to the cook whenever
we could.
After eatin' moldy bacon, they sure tasted
good.
Mitchell was talking in a loud voice one day,
To his horse that wouldn't do a thing the right
way,
You blankety-blank! Now I guess you'll go,
You old Blan—there's a hun of a rabbit,
whoa!
From then 'twas a byword, the boys all got
the habit,
Of saying at everything, "Whoa, there's a
hun of a rabbit."
The rattle snakes were thick. At first that
seemed strange.
We never say a rattler on our own home
range.
So with heavy quirts we had lots of battles,
And when we left we each of us had a to-
bacco can of rattles.
Rattlers were as new to our horses as they
were to us boys,
But the horse seemed to know by instinct
when he heard that threatening noise
Got so he'd swap ends at anything that
sounded like a buzz,
And start out the other direction like a real
good cowhorse does.
And if you happened to be a sleepy cowboy
settin' on his back.
You'd wake up to find he'd come mighty
close to slippin' from under his pack.
Harry and I went hunting one day, For a rab-
bit or sage hen that might get in our way.
We went down a couple of ridges apart,
'bout half a mile,
When I looked over where Harry was I had
to stop and smile,
He was goin' thru such funny antics, I
thought he was havin' a fit.
Then I got scared, I happened to think he
might have got snake bit.
So I rode over to him and what do you think
I found?

He had a big rattle snake pinned down on
the ground,
With a rock on its tail and its head swayin'
high,
Harry was spittin' tobacco juice right at its
eye.
Or tryin' to hit its mouth which was open and
a hissin'.
He was trying hard, but just the same was
every time a missin'
Then I got down and tried to too, but it wasn't
any use,
That snake was sure a good one at dodgin'
tobacco juice.
One evening we had company and they
were welcome too,
They stayed 'till nearly midnight, as old
friends sometimes do.
The boys that came were Aden Webb, Gus
Darcy, and Alex Dunbar.
They too had a shipment of cattle and had
come out there to meet it,
But it was there and all they did was to un-
load the cars and beat it.
They camped two miles below us, next
morning we saw their dust,
And when we saw it start toward home, we
thot it a little unjust.
But it wasn't much later that our last ship-
ment came in,
And our slow trip home we were glad to
begin.
The morning we were leaving that well worn
first camp ground,
A herd of sheep came down the draw and
kind of circled 'round.
Al and I stopped to watch them, they were
quite a ways away.
The dog took our eye, he seemed to know
just what the herder'd say.
When the herder whistled, he'd circle the
band,
Then back he'd come again, when the Mexi-
can waved his hand.
That looked good to Al and me,
And we thought we'd whistle, just to see
If the dog would work for everyone.
And boy! He shot out and did he run,
Around them woolies away out wide,
The herder waved and stamped and cried.
When the dog would stop to look about,

Another whistle from us would start him out.
Till the sheep went wild and the herder too,
And the poor dog didn't know what to do.
Then we rode on and we lost no sleep,
'Bout the rattled dog and the crazy sheep.
By this time a lot of little calves had come
along,
And as some of them weren't so very strong,
Harry got out and bought a team and a
wagon,
So we could give the little chaps a ride when
they got to draggin'.
Mitch was elected to drive this baby cart,
And he was peeved about it, right from the
start.
So when we found a tired calf and had to
do the trick,
We'd dump him in the wagon and get away
right quick.
That night when Mitch got into camp and
started to unload,
He didn't have a single calf, they'd jumped
out on the road.
Big Sage Creek was our camp that night.
By dark it was rainin' and sure was a fright.
The cattle were restless and wandered
around,
Till Harry ordered all of us out on the bed
ground.
And spite of us all, the night was so black,
That about twenty-five cows got away and
started back.
And six head of horses started on ahead.
Clarence brought them back next morning.
They were sure homesick, he said,
the lost cows were rounded up by some of
the other men,
And we were soon all started out on our way
again.
At Saratoga we counted, and a few cows
short we found.
So Harry sent McAvoy and me back as far
as our first camp ground.
To find the lost ones and brand 'em and
leave 'em, that was all,
Then he'd send a rep to pick 'em up and
bring 'em home in the fall.
By the time we'd caught and branded 'em,
my horse was plumb played out,
That I'd travel for a while some other way,
there wasn't any doubt.

There was no use fight'n the poor old chap,
So I unsaddled and hobbled him with a latigo
strap.
We weren't very far from where we'd had
our first camp,
So I picked up my saddle and started to
tramp.
Fred went on to Nevins' and said that he
would send
A horse back to me next day if they had one
to lend.
I walked along in the dark 'till I came to a
spring.
Where I decided to camp when I heard a
bell ring.
'Twas a sheep bell's tinkle, then I thought
about
The band that pulled in just as we pulled
out.
There might be a chance to get a place to
sleep.
So I shouldered my saddle and went look-
ing for the sheep.
I found them, but they'd never seen a
saddled man in the dark,
And they started to run, an' the herder came
out an' the dogs began to bark.
Then some shots rang out, he was shootin'
in the air,
To scare coyotes away 'fore he knew I was
there
Well, I was wishin' it was a coyote and that
I was back at the spring,
Or any place else, just so I was where I
couldn't hear them bullets sing.
It might have been all right, but, gee, I
couldn't tell,
Where the darn Mex was shootin', so I
started in to yell.
When he discovered me and I told him of
my plight,
He took me into his sheepwagon where it
was plenty light.
It seemed he'd had some troubles, I guess
he didn't lie,
For he said right straight at me as he looked
me in the eye,
"Some punchers whistle at my dog, he put
my sheep on the run.
You don't know who do it? The son of a gun."
Which just goes to show you never can tell,

Where you sins will catch up to you this side
of —Hades.
Now if I'd told him the truth, it's a cinch he'd
never known,
The pleasure of my company and he looked
so alone.
So I gave him my sympathy, said it was just
too bad,
A dirty Irish trick, and I tried to look sad.
I guess I succeeded for he took me in,
And never mentioned the subject again.
Next day I went to get my horse, but he still
wasn't right,
So I led him back to sheep camp and we
both stayed there that night.
Next morning he seemed pretty lively and
we started back over the hill.
The herder watched us out of sight with a
friendly "Adios, Bill".
Fred had passed the sheep camp when he
left me that night ,
so he figured I'd get that far and he knew I'd
be all right.
Well, a little later on, Fred and I got together
again
And we jogged on down the dusty road, 'till
we caught the other men.
Then we trailed the cows homeward without much strife,
Just the everyday events of a cowboys life,
A pushin' 'em along with a yip and a yow,
With the end of your draggin' rope, pickin'
up a lazy cow.
Catchin' tired calves and puttin' 'em in the
wagon for a ride,
sometimes cussin', sometimes singin',
sweat a smearin' yer dusty hide.
Gatherin' round the old chuckwagon 'n the
evenin' tired enough
That it sounds like songs from heaven when
the cook sings out "hot stuff",
Then night herdin' in the starlight, sometimes so quiet you heard
The tired breathing of the cattle, then the
twitter of a bird.
As you watch the sky grow lighter in the east
and see day break.
And you roll another cigarette just to keep
yourself awake.

Then some nights it's dark and stormy, cattle
start at thunder crash,
And you watch out for bunch quitters by the
glare of lightning flash.
Then at last one day we came in sight of
dear old North Park land,
We held the bunch where Wyatts live now,
and took some home to brand.
Mitch and I day herded, but the cows were
pretty meek,
And one day we went swimmin' in Cana-
dian Creek.
After the kicking and the splashing was done
We crawled out on the bank toe dry in the
sun.
I raised my arm just to scratch my head,
When Mitch looked around at me and said,
"Why you—" Well, he said what I was, and
just what I had,
He said it with trimmin's and he seemed real
mad.
You see we'd been bed partners all the way,
Except the night or two I'd hit the
sheepherder's hay.
That generous Mex, he was sure no hog,
He was even with me for rattlin' his dog.
But you'd a thought Mitch was King or some-
thing as nice,
Kicking up such a row 'bout a few little —
wood ticks.
Well, I took a bath in strong sheep dip,
And Mitch treated me white the rest of the
trip.
With the cows all branded and ready to
roam,
We took them over to Middle Park to their
summer home.
'Till we brought them back to winter hay with
the roundup in the Fall.
And now my story's ended, Hope I haven't
been a bore,
But that's the way I saw it; Thank you for
listening in,
And I'd give a lot of what I own and of what
I hope to win,
To experience once more the sorrows and
joys
Of life on the range with those same cow-
boys!